Instructor's Manual and Test Questions

to accompany

The Power of Critical Thinking

Effective Reasoning About Ordinary and Extraordinary Claims

Lewis Vaughn

New York   Oxford

OXFORD UNIVERSITY PRESS

2005

Oxford University Press

Oxford   New York
Auckland   Bangkok   Buenos Aires   Cape Town   Chennai
Dar es Salaam   Delhi   Hong Kong   Istanbul   Karachi   Kolkata
Kuala Lumpur   Madrid   Melbourne   Mexico City   Mumbai   Nairobi
São Paulo   Shanghai   Taipei   Tokyo   Toronto

Copyright © 2005 by Oxford University Press, Inc.

Published by Oxford University Press, Inc.
198 Madison Avenue, New York, New York 10016
www.oup.com

Oxford is a registered trademark of Oxford University Press

ISBN-13: 978-0-19-522359-0
ISBN-10: 0-19-522359-4

Printing number: 9 8 7 6 5 4 3 2 1

Printed in the United States of America
on acid-free paper

Contents

Introduction

This text incorporates a number of features that should help make teaching a course in critical thinking a little easier. Even better, there is enough flexibility built into the book to help make teaching *your preferred kind of course* a little easier. At least this is the strategy behind much of the text's content, organization, and pedagogy. Only the brave who must stand before students who know nothing of critical thinking can say if the teaching burden has been lightened.

USING THE MODULAR STRUCTURE

The text can be easily adapted to different kinds of courses because the chapters are, for the most part, modular. The chapters can be taught in almost any order. Possible exceptions are Chapters 3 and 9. Chapter 3 is a good introduction to the chapters on deductive reasoning (Chapters 6 and 7). You may skip Chapter 3 and go straight to Chapters 6 and 7, but students may find it rough going at first. On the other hand, a critical thinking course that employed Chapter 3 as its only foray into the fundamentals of argument (and therefore skipping Chapters 6, 7, and 8) would still give students a good grounding in argument basics. Chapter 9 is necessary for full appreciation of Chapters 10 and 11. But even without 9, students will still benefit from exposure to 10 and 11.

Here are some of the possible course configurations:

- To teach a course in **basic reasoning skills**: Chapters 1-5 and 9.
- To teach a course emphasizing **traditional logic**: Chapters 1-8.
- To teach a critical thinking course emphasizing **writing**, or a **writing** course emphasizing critical thinking: Chapters 1-5 (including all the writing modules) and 9 and 10.
- To teach a critical thinking course emphasizing **science**: Chapters 1-4 and 8-10.
- To teach a course emphasizing how critical reasoning can be applied to **practical problems** in real life: Chapters 2-5 and 9-11.

USING THE WRITING MODULES

In this text, material on writing essays (or essay questions) is relegated to four writing lessons, or modules. There is one writing module at the end of each of Chapters 1-4. Each one is designed to help the student think about, plan, and write good argumentative essays—and to do so with a minimum of instructor input. The modules are progressive, starting in Chapter 1 with a few fundamentals of the writing process then later (in Chapters 2, 3, and 4) covering basic guidelines and concepts that can help students think critically and write intelligently about arguments and issues. The modules are modular though progressive. They can be used at any point in the course or not used at all. Their main purpose, however, is to help instructors get students writing as early as possible, progressing rapidly to more challenging writing assignments—without stopping the course to teach a chapter on writing.

USING THE BOXES

There are many text boxes here. They come in three varieties: (1) Review Notes (boxes that reiterate the main points of chapter sections); (2) Highlights of Previous Chapters (summaries of the key points of the preceding chapters); and (3) Further Thought (boxes that provide additional, sometimes humorous, material on a topic and challenge students to think). The Further Thought boxes can be used in a variety of ways:

- The topic of a box can be used as the basis for some lively discussions about interesting or fun issues relating to the chapter material.
- Students can be asked to evaluate the claim or argument presented in a box
- The boxes can be used just as the end-of-text readings are—as short essays to evaluate in a paper.
- Students can be asked to do some online research on some aspect of a box's topic. The results could be the subject of a short paper, a report presented in class, or the topic of a class discussion.

USING THE INTEGRATIVE EXERCISES

Each chapter (except the first) has a set of "integrative" exercises. These are exercise sets that overlap with material in previous chapters. For example, integrative exercises for Chapter 5 will include some exercises that pertain to material in Chapters 1 through 4 as well as 5. The point is to avoid the problem of students not being able to see how the various aspects of critical thinking fit together. In most cases, integrative exercises serve as reviews of all previous chapters. In the later chapters, they review only selected previous chapters. The chapters covered are indicated in each set of exercises. Integrative exercises from several chapters can also be combined to serve as a section or mid-term exam or as a review for such an exam.

For this text, integrative exercises are a major aid to student review of material. But the online Student Guide is also helpful—and might even turn out to be the students' preferred source of review material. The study guide provides the following for each chapter: chapter summary, chapter objectives, study questions, multiple-choice review quiz, true/false review quiz, chapter glossary, answers to selected exercises in the text, bonus exercises, and Web links.

USING THE READINGS

The readings at the back of the book can be put to work in several ways. They are, of course, used in the four writing modules (Chapters 1-4) as well as the end-of-chapter writing assignments for Chapters 5-11. Each chapter's writing assignment deals with a different reading selection. Almost all of the readings, however, can be used in writing exercises in any chapter. In most of the writing exercises, students are asked to write a paper to evaluate the claims, arguments, or theories offered in an essay. In a variation on this, students are asked to rewrite an essay to repair a faulty argument or to devise a better one.

One interesting approach is to ask students to devise their own questions regarding the readings. Students can exchange their questions and write extended answers to them. The questions can also be exchanged in class and used as the starting point for discussions.

ABOUT THE WEBSITE

A Companion Website for *The Power of Critical Thinking* is available at **www.oup.com/us/criticalthinking**. Students will find detailed chapter summaries, study questions, self-correcting review quizzes, and glossary term flashcards. The answers to selected exercises unanswered in the text are also posted here. (The full set of answers to exercises not answered in the text is provided in this Instructor's Manual.) For both students and instructors, there are Web Links to sites with food for thought relevant to chapter content. Finally, instructors may access several sample syllabi and the PowerPoint Lecture Guide (the contents of which are outlined at the end of this Instructor's Manual).

Chapter 1
The Power of Critical Thinking

In teaching a course in critical thinking, instructors face two large problems right off—students don't know what critical thinking is, and they don't know why it matters. The objectives of this initial chapter, then, are (1) to provide students with a clear and readable preface to critical thinking fundamentals and (2) to explain how critical thinking intersects with their lives and why this intersection deserves their attention. Thus, this chapter is the gateway to the rest of the book. Without thoroughly understanding the basic ideas in this chapter, students will probably find most of the other chapters more difficult than need be.

To meet objective 1, the chapter is pitched to students who have no inkling of critical thinking. It begins with a working definition of critical thinking and explains and illustrates the basic concepts of *statement*, *argument*, *premise*, *conclusion*, *inference*, and *indicator words*. There is also ample material on distinguishing arguments from nonarguments and picking arguments out of extended passages. The chapter is purposely short to avoid overwhelming students and deliberately concise and straightforward (without being simplistic) to ensure complete understanding. The chapter, nevertheless, is long on opportunities for students to practice their new skills through the exercises and writing assignments. Some instructors (maybe most?) are not afraid to spend two, three, or more weeks on such fundamentals. With this chapter under their belts, students should be able to jump off to the more demanding chapters—to Chapter 3, for instance, or perhaps even to Chapters 6 and 7, probably the most daunting for first-time students.

To meet objective 2, Chapter 1 explains the importance of critical thinking primarily by zeroing in on a recurrent theme: In large measure, the quality of our lives is defined by the quality of our thinking—and the quality of our thinking can be improved through the use of critical thinking. The question put to students then is not whether they sometimes use critical thinking (we all do), but how well they use it.

This line, of course, may not get very far with students if they harbor prejudices against the very idea of critical thinking. They may, for example, think that critical thinking makes people excessively critical or cynical, emotionally cold, and creatively constrained. So these notions are examined and dispatched in short order.

The first writing tutorial (module) appears at the end of this chapter. The modules are progressive, and so this one starts at square one—with an introduction to the purpose and structure of argumentative essays and a step-by-step procedure for writing them. Module 1 helps students put arguments in essay form, giving them another way to practice analyzing and presenting arguments.

One useful approach to argument analysis is to have students write out an argument in short essay form, then have them exchange papers and identify the premises and conclusions. At this point it probably is not premature to have the students decide whether they accept the conclusions and explain why or why not.

CHAPTER SUMMARY

Critical thinking is the systematic evaluation or formulation of beliefs, or statements, by rational standards. Critical thinking is *systematic* because it involves distinct procedures and methods. It entails *evaluation* and *formulation* because it's used to both assess existing beliefs (yours or someone else's) and devise new ones. And it operates according to *reasonable standards* in that beliefs are judged according to the reasons and reasoning that support them.

Critical thinking matters because our lives are defined by our actions and choices, and our actions and choices are guided by our thinking. Critical thinking helps guide us toward beliefs that are worthy of acceptance, that can help us be successful in life, however we define success.

A consequence of not thinking critically is a loss of personal freedom. If you passively accept beliefs that have been handed to you by your family and your culture, then those beliefs are not really yours. If they are not really yours, and you let them guide your choices and actions, then they—not you—are in charge of your life. Your beliefs are yours only if you critically examine them for yourself to see if they are supported by good reasons.

Some people believe that critical thinking will make them cynical, emotionally cold, and creatively constrained. But there is no good reason to believe that this is the case. Critical thinking does not necessarily lead to cynicism. It can complement our feelings by helping us sort them out. And it doesn't limit creativity—it helps perfect it.

Critical thinking is a rational, systematic process that we apply to beliefs of all kinds. As we use the term here, *belief* is just another word for statement, or claim. A *statement* is an assertion that something is or is not the case. When you're engaged in critical thinking, you are mostly either evaluating a statement or trying to formulate one. In both cases your primary task is to figure out how strongly to believe the statement (based on how likely it is to be true). The strength of your belief will depend on the strength of the reasons in favor of the statement.

In critical thinking an argument is not a feud but a set of statements—statements supposedly providing reasons for accepting another statement. The statements given in support of another statement are called the *premises*. The statement that the premises are used to support is called the *conclusion*. An argument then is a group of statements in which some of them (the premises) are intended to support another of them (the conclusion).

Being able to identify arguments is an important skill on which many other critical thinking skills are based. The task is made easier by indicator words that frequently accompany arguments and signal that a premise or conclusion is present. Premise indicators include *for*, *since*, and *because*. Conclusion indicators include *so, therefore*, and *thus*.

Arguments almost never appear neatly labeled for identification. They usually come imbedded in a lot of statements that are not part of the arguments. Arguments can be complex and lengthy. Your main challenge is to identify the conclusion and premises without getting lost in all the other verbiage.

EXERCISES NOT ANSWERED IN THE TEXT

Exercise 1-1

2. Critical thinking is primarily concerned with *how* you think.
3. Critical thinking is systematic because it involves distinct procedures and methods.

5. If you passively accept beliefs that have been handed to you by your parents, your culture, or your teachers, then those beliefs are not really yours. If they are not really yours, and you let them guide your choices and actions, then they—not you—are in charge of your life.

7. Critical thinking can also help us clarify our feelings and deal with them more effectively. Our emotions often need the guidance of reason. Likewise, our reasoning needs our emotions. It is our feelings that motivate us to action, and without motivation our reasoning would never get off the ground.

9. Critical thinking is essential. Is critical thinking essential?

10. We should proportion our acceptance of a statement according to the reasons in its favor.

12. If the accident happened at 5:00 p.m., it was John's fault. The accident did happen at 5:00 p.m. So it was his fault.

13. A premise is a statement given in support of another statement.

15. An argument requires reasons that support a conclusion; the mere assertion of a belief does not provide reasons.

16. False

18. Yes

20. Therefore; consequently; so

21. Because; since; for

22. The poll suggests that most people are happy. Therefore, most of them are happy.

24. False

Exercise 1-2

2. No statement
3. Statement
5. No statement
6. No statement
8. Statement
9. Statement

Exercise 1-3

2. No argument
3. No argument
5. No argument
6. No argument
8. Argument. Conclusion: Jesus loves me.
9. Argument. Conclusion: Spiderman is a better superhero than Superman.
10. Argument. Conclusion: Whether our argument concerns public affairs or some other subject we must know some, if not all, of the facts about the subject on which we are to speak and argue.
12. Argument. Conclusion: If someone says something that offends me, I should have the right to stop that kind of speech.
13. Argument. Conclusion: Citizens who so value their "independence" that they will not enroll in a political party are really forfeiting independence.
14. Argument. Conclusion: If someone says something that offends me, I cannot and should not try to stop them from speaking.

16. Argument. Conclusion: The U.S. government cannot be trusted when it comes to sending our children to war.

Exercise 1-4

2. Argument. Conclusion: Therefore, you are not fit to serve in your current capacity. Premise: You have neglected your duty on several occasions. Premise: You have been absent from work too many times.
3. No argument
5. No argument
6. Argument. Conclusion: Current-day Christians use violence to spread their right-to-life message. Premise: These Christians, often referred to as the religious right, are well known for violent demonstrations against Planned Parenthood and other abortion clinics. Premise: Doctors and other personnel are threatened with death. Premise: Clinics have been bombed. Premise: There have even been cases of doctors being murdered.
8. No argument
9. Argument: Conclusion: Witches are real. Premise: They are mentioned in the Bible. Premise: There are many people today who claim to be witches. Premise: And historical records reveal that there were witches in Salem.
11. Argument. Conclusion: Therefore, Vaughn's car is ready for the junk yard. Premise: Vaughn's car is old. Premise: It is beat up. Premise: It is unsafe to drive.

Exercise 1-5

1. Premise: Strong family values have been shown to decrease crime rates. Premise: Poverty, political conflict, and deficit spending are all caused by a lack of family values.
2. Premise: Any creature that can suffer pain has moral rights. Premise: All animals can suffer pain.
4. Premise: Later I realized that I had completely lost track of time. Premise: I felt as if I was frozen forever.
5. Premise: All suffering humans have the right to end their own lives. Premise: All medical patients suffer in some way.
7. Premise: The media are reporting that there are suspicions regarding the financial dealings of Governor Spendthrift. Premise: Many people in state government say that they are suspicious of the governor's financial dealings.
8. Premise: The FBI and CIA say that the Internet is a terrorist's most dangerous weapon. Premise: Terrorists say that their most dangerous weapon is the Internet.
10. Premise: Scientific studies have shown that pornography educates people about sexuality. Premise: Societies that use pornography are the most highly educated about sexuality.
11. Premise: Scientific studies have shown that pornography always misleads people about sexuality. Premise: The more pornography a person uses, the more ignorant they are about sexuality.
13. Premise: It is the duty of every student to prevent any arbitrary decisions by the administration. Premise: This tuition increase is an arbitrary decision by the administration.
14. Premise: After having two drinks, Ling passes out. Premise: Ling is completely drunk after one drink.

7

Exercise 1-6

1. Conclusion: You will fall if you climb a tree.
3. Conclusion: School vouchers have improved the quality of education in four states.
5. Conclusion: Edgar will be very happy.
6. Conclusion: There is no morality.
7. Conclusion: Life has meaning.
9. Conclusion: Nancy cannot be trusted.

Exercise 1-7

2. Conclusion: [Francis Bacon] is the father of experimental philosophy. Premise: Before Chancellor Bacon, no one had any idea of experimental philosophy. Premise: Of an infinity of experiments which have been made since his time, there is hardly a single one which has not been pointed out in his book.
4. Conclusion: Moral subjectivism has some rather bizarre consequences. Premise: For one thing, it implies that each of us is morally infallible. (As long as we approve of or believe in what we are doing, we can do no wrong.) Premise: But we cannot be morally infallible.

TEST BANK

Multiple Choice
(Correct answers are marked with an asterisk.)

1. Critical thinking is systematic because it…
   a. Is caused by a state of mind
   b. Has practical implications
   * c. Involves distinct procedures and methods
   d. Leads to better understanding

2. A belief is worth accepting if…
   a. It is consistent with our needs
   b. It has not been proven wrong
   c. It is accepted by our peers
   * d. We have good reasons to accept it

3. The word *critical* in critical thinking refers to…
   * a. Using careful judgment or judicious evaluation
   b. A faultfinding attitude
   c. Attempts to win an argument
   d. A lack of respect for other people

4. An assertion that something is or is not the case is known as a(n)...
    a. Predicate
    b. Premise
    c. Argument
    * d. Statement

5. Statements backed by good reasons are...
    a. To be believed with certainty
    * b. Worthy of strong acceptance
    c. Beyond doubt
    d. Deserving of weak acceptance

6. A group of statements in which some of them (the premises) are intended to support another of them (the conclusion) is known as a(n)...
    a. Chain argument
    b. Claim
    * c. Argument
    d. Reason

7. Words that frequently accompany arguments and signal that a premise or conclusion is present are known as...
    *a. Indicator words
    b. Premises
    c. Indicator verbs
    d. Argument components

8. Probably the best advice for anyone trying to uncover or dissect arguments is...
    a. Find the premises first
    b. Paraphrase the argument
    c. Determine the truth of premises
    *d. Find the conclusion first

9. The function of an explanation is to...
    a. Try to prove that a statement is true
    * b. Try to show why or how something is the way it is
    c. Try to show that something is the case
    d. Try to show that a statement is in dispute

10. According to the text, if you passively accept beliefs that have been handed to you by your culture, then those beliefs are...
    a. Worthy of acceptance
    * b. Not really yours
    c. Critically examined
    d. Worthy of rejection

True/False
(Correct answers marked with an asterisk.)

1. The fundamental concern of critical thinking is the cause of your beliefs.
   a. True
   *b. False

2. In critical thinking, beliefs are evaluated by how well they are supported by reasons.
   *a. True
   b. False

3. Critical thinking makes you cynical and unimaginative.
   a. True
   *b. False

4. Critical thinking can go hand in hand with creativity because it can be used to assess and enhance the creation.
   * a. True
   b. False

5. Statements, or claims, are either true, false, or neutral
   a. True
   * b. False

6. Common conclusion indicators include *for*, *given that*, and *for the reason that*.
   a. True
   * b. False

7. In critical thinking, argument refers to a quarrel or debate.
   a. True
   *b. False

8. Statements given in support of another statement are called premises.
   *a. True
   b. False

9. A declaration of beliefs can sometimes constitute an argument.
   a. True
   *b. False

10 In good arguments, premises are always explicit.
   a. True
   *b. False

Short Answer/Short Essay

1. How does logic differ from critical thinking?

2. Why is it important to critically examine your beliefs?

3. How do critical thinking and emotions complement one another?

4. What does it mean to say that "critical thinking perfects the creation"?

5. What is the difference between sentences that do and do not express statements?

6. What is the role of reasons in critical thinking?

7. What are indicator words and how can they help you identify an argument?

8. How does an explanation differ from an argument?

9. What is probably the best advice for anyone trying to evaluate an argument? What is the rationale behind this advice?

10. What are some of the most common variations in the structure of arguments?

Chapter 2
The "Environment" of Critical Thinking

As every instructor knows, it's tough to teach the basics of critical thinking to students who have never before been exposed to the subject. But their lack of previous experience with the subject is only part of the challenge of getting them to understand and appreciate critical thinking. Students are often not merely clueless about critical thinking; they may have the deck stacked against them at the outset because they harbor assumptions, prejudices, and habits of mind that impede clear thinking. (The impediments thrown up by logical fallacies are mostly a separate matter, taken up in Chapter 5.) The purpose of this chapter, then, is to address some of these hindrances—to help students become aware of common ways in which their thinking can run off the tracks. The premise here is that awareness is half the battle.

So almost all of the exercises are meant to raise awareness. The Field Problems—and your own similar projects or group discussions—should be extremely useful in encouraging student introspection. They suggest some ways that students can critique their own thinking or that of others without feeling self-conscious or making others uncomfortable. Writing assignments can also be put to work for the same reasons.

CHAPTER SUMMARY

Critical thinking takes place in a mental environment consisting of our experiences, thoughts, and feelings. Some elements in this inner environment can sabotage our efforts to think critically or at least make critical thinking more difficult. Fortunately, we can exert some control over these elements. With practice, we can detect errors in our thinking, restrain attitudes and feelings that can disrupt our reasoning, and achieve enough objectivity to make critical thinking possible.

The most common of these hindrances to critical thinking fall into two main categories: (1) Those obstacles that crop up because of *how* we think and (2) those that occur because of *what* we think. The first category is comprised of psychological factors such as our fears, attitudes, motivations, and desires. The second category is made up of certain philosophical beliefs.

None of us is immune to the psychological obstacles. Among them are the products of egocentric thinking. We may accept a claim solely because it advances our interests or just because it helps us save face. To overcome these pressures, we must (1) be aware of strong emotions that can warp our thinking, (2) be alert to ways that critical thinking can be undermined, and (3) ensure that we take into account *all* relevant factors when we evaluate a claim.

The first category of hindrances also includes those that arise because of group pressure. These obstacles include conformist pressures from groups that we belong to and ethnocentric urges to think that our group is superior to others. The best defense against group pressure is to proportion our beliefs according to the strength of reasons.

We may also have certain core beliefs that can undermine critical thinking (the second category of hindrances). Subjective relativism is the view that truth depends solely on what someone believes—a notion that may make critical thinking look superfluous. But subjective relativism leads to some strange consequences. For example, if the doctrine were true, each of us would be infallible. Also, subjective relativism has a logical problem—it's self-defeating. Its truth implies its falsity. There are no good reasons to accept this form of relativism.

Social relativism is the view that truth is relative to societies—a claim that would also seem to make critical thinking unnecessary. But this notion is undermined by the same kinds of problems that plague subjective relativism.

Philosophical skepticism is the doctrine that we know much less than we think we do. One form of philosophical skepticism says that we cannot know anything unless the belief is beyond all possible doubt. But this is not a plausible criterion for knowledge. To be knowledge, claims need not be beyond all possible doubt, but beyond all *reasonable* doubt.

EXERCISES NOT ANSWERED IN THE TEXT

Exercise 2-1

2. Those hindrances that arise because of *how* we think and those that occur because of *what* we think.
3. Clifford asserts that it is morally wrong to believe a proposition without justification or evidence.
4. Drawing conclusions about people without sufficient reasons.
6. To save face, we may accept or defend claims just to protect our image—blaming others for our mistakes, trying to justify our unjustifiable behavior, or failing to admit error.
8. The rule of thumb is: If you sense a rush of emotions when you deal with a particular issue, stop. Think about what's happening and why. Then continue at a slower pace and with greater attention to the basics of critical reasoning, double-checking to ensure that you are not ignoring or suppressing evidence or getting sloppy in your evaluations.
9. A kind of biased thinking in which we notice certain things and ignore others, even though we should be noticing both.
10. We may ignore facts that contradict our beliefs and search out facts that support them.
12. The group pressure that comes from presuming that our own group is the best and all other groups are not as good.
13. The fallacy of arguing that a claim must be true merely because a substantial number of people believe it.
15. The idea that truth depends on what someone believes.
16. In large part, critical thinking is about determining whether statements are true or false. But if we can make a statement true just by believing it to be true, then critical thinking would seem to be unnecessary.
18. The view that truth is relative to societies.
19. The view that we know much less than we think we do or nothing at all.
20. It seems that our knowledge does not require certainty, for we seem to know many things even though we do not have absolutely conclusive reasons.

Exercise 2-2

2. Self-interested thinking
3. Self-interested thinking
5. Group pressure

6. Group pressure
8. Self-interested thinking
9. Group pressure
11. Group pressure

Exercise 2-3

2. a, b
4. None
5. d
7. b

Exercise 2-4

2. peer pressure; possible negative consequences: harm to John's health and reputation, legal problems due to John's illegal drug use
4. either peer pressure or appeal to popularity; possible negative consequences: damage to Yang Lei's integrity
5. possible we-are-better pressure; possible negative consequences: injustice to Alex, loss of Alex's talent to the school
6. appeal to popularity; possible negative consequences: damage to Sylvia's integrity, establishment of a precedent in which columnists cave in to intolerance

Exercise 2-5

3. face-saving; possible negative consequences: Antonio's self-deception, which may lead to further poor performance
4. face-saving and perhaps other kinds of self-interest; possible negative consequences: unethical professional behavior, which could ruin her career, mislead both scientists and the public about the treatment, and put people at risk for the treatment's side effects.
5. Face-saving; possible negative consequences: dishonesty, which misleads people and sets Max up for self-deception or future dishonesty

TEST BANK

Multiple Choice
(Correct answers are marked with an asterisk.)

1. Category 1 obstacles to critical thinking are those that come into play because of ...
   a. Logical considerations
   b. Physical impediments
   * c. Psychological factors
   d. Deductive concerns

2. We push our self-interested thinking too far when we…
   a. Use inductive reasoning
   b. Reject claims after examining them
   * c. Accept claims for no good reason
   d. Think for ourselves

3. A guideline that is NOT likely to help you escape self-interested thinking is…
   a. Watch out when things get personal
   * b. Tell people what they want to hear
   c. Be alert to ways that critical thinking can be undermined
   d. Ensure that nothing has been left out

4. Philosopher Bertrand Russell claimed that the passionate holding of an opinion is a sure sign of…
   a. Critical thinking
   b. Careful evaluation of evidence
   * c. A lack of reasons to support the opinion
   d. A deference to the opinions of others

5. Statements backed by good reasons are…
   a. To be believed with certainty
   * b. Worthy of strong acceptance
   c. Beyond doubt
   d. Deserving of weak acceptance

6. A common flaw in reasoning is the failure to consider evidence or arguments that…
   * a. Do not support preferred claims or positions
   b. Support preferred evidence or arguments
   c. Are familiar or predictable
   d. We have held previously

7. Words that frequently accompany arguments and signal that a premise or conclusion is present are known as…
   *a. Indicator words
   b. Premises
   c. Indicator verbs
   d. Argument components

8. Drawing conclusions about people without sufficient reasons is known as…
   a. Appeal to common practice
   b. Appeal to tradition
   c. Peer pressure
   *d. Stereotyping

9. Subjective relativism is the idea that …
    a. Truth is relative to societies
    * b. Truth depends on what someone believes
    c. There is a way the world is
    d. Some objective truths are about our subjective states

10. Self-interested thinking can leave you vulnerable to…
    a. Well established claims
    b. Self-examination and self-denial
    * c. Propaganda and manipulation
    d. The needs of others

True/False
(Correct answers marked with an asterisk.)

1. The idea that we each create our own reality involves a logical contradiction.
    * a. True
    b. False

2. Subjective relativism implies that we are all fallible.
    a. True
    * b. False

3. According to the text, knowledge requires certainty.
    a. True
    *b. False

4. Doubt is always possible, but it is not always reasonable.
    * a. True
    b. False

5. Psychological impediments to critical thinking are rare.
    a. True
    * b. False

6. There is something inherently wrong with accepting a claim that furthers your own interests.
    a. True
    *b. False

7. Emotional protestations and rejections of all relevant evidence often signal the influence of self-interest on our thinking.
    * a. True
    b. False

8. A common flaw in reasoning is the failure to take relative truth into account.
   a. True
   * b. False

9. The remedy for the problem of selective attention is to make a conscious effort to look for supporting evidence.
   a. True
   * b. False

10. Group thinking can generate narrow-mindedness, resistance to change, and stereotyping.
    * a. True
    b. False

Short Answer/Short Essay

1. What are the two main categories of common obstacles to critical thinking?

2. According to the text, what influence might face-saving have on your thinking?

3. What are the three guidelines for overcoming the excessive influence of self-interested thinking and how might you use them?

4. How might a critical thinker counteract the phenomenon of selective attention?

5. What is the appeal to popularity and how can it adversely affect critical thinking?

6. According to the text, what's wrong with passively accepting the beliefs that we are given?

7. Do you accept the idea that it is immoral to believe claims without good evidence? Why or why not?

8. Are you a subjective relativist? Why or why not?

9. How have philosophers responded to the challenge of philosophical skepticism?

10. How does the notion that we each create our own reality involve a logical contradiction?

Chapter 3
Making Sense of Arguments

This chapter covers all the most important skills and concepts involved in identifying, evaluating, and diagramming arguments. It therefore can serve as a stand-alone introduction to arguments, providing enough essential content to occupy a good part of a semester. A critical thinking course that employed this chapter as its only foray into the fundamentals of argument (and therefore skipping Chapters 6, 7, and 8) could still be substantial, especially if all the exercises and other opportunities to practice skills were fully used. (The online Student Guide and the writing modules could play a large role.) Alternatively, for instructors who want to teach a course that's heavier on argument and traditional logic, this chapter could serve as a good prelude to the later chapters on categorical logic, propositional logic, and inductive reasoning.

CHAPTER SUMMARY

Arguments come in two forms: deductive and inductive. A deductive argument is intended to provide logically conclusive support for a conclusion; an inductive one, probable support for a conclusion. Deductive arguments can be valid or invalid; inductive arguments, strong or weak. A valid argument with true premises is said to be sound. A strong argument with true premises is said to be cogent.

Evaluating an argument is the most important skill of critical thinking. It involves finding the conclusion and premises, checking to see if the argument is deductive or inductive, determining its validity or strength, and discovering if the premises are true or false. Sometimes you also have to ferret out implicit, or unstated, premises.

Arguments can come in certain common patterns, or forms. Two valid forms that you will often run into are *modus ponens* (affirming the antecedent) and *modus tollens* (denying the consequent). Two common invalid forms are denying the antecedent and affirming the consequent.

Analyzing the structure of arguments is easier if you diagram them. Argument diagrams can help you visualize the function of premises and conclusions and the relationships among complex arguments with several subarguments.

Assessing very long arguments can be challenging because they may contain lots of verbiage but few or no arguments, and many premises can be implicit. Evaluating long arguments, though, requires the same basic steps as assessing short ones: (1) Ensure that you understand the argument, (2) locate the conclusion, (3) find the premises, and (4) diagram it to clarify logical relationships.

EXERCISES NOT ANSWERED IN THE TEXT

Exercise 3-1

1. An argument intended to provide logically conclusive support for its conclusion.
2. An argument intended to provide probable, not conclusive, support for its conclusion.

3. Inductive arguments are not truth preserving, for it is possible for the premises in a strong inductive argument to be true while the conclusion is false.

5. A deductively valid argument has the kind of logical structure that guarantees the truth of the conclusion if the premises are true.

6. No; an inductive argument is intended to provide only probable support for its conclusion.

7. An inductive argument that succeeds in providing probable—but not conclusive—logical support for its conclusion is said to be strong. An inductive argument that fails to provide such support is said to be weak.

9. Cogent

10. Yes; yes

11. At least one of the premises is false.

13. Conclusions of deductive arguments are absolute in that either the conclusion is true, or it is not. There is no sliding scale of truth or falsity.

Exercise 3-2

1. Step 1: *Conclusion*: Jack is lying; *Premises*: Either Jack is lying or he is not. If his ears turn red, he's lying. If they don't turn red, he's telling the truth. His ears are red.
Step 2: Deductively valid
Step 3: Does not apply
Step 4: Does not apply

3. Step 1: *Conclusion*: You're nuts; *Premises*: If you go to that party you're completely nuts. You're going to the party.
Step 2: Deductively valid
Step 3: Does not apply
Step 4: Does not apply

4. Step 1: *Conclusion*: Good sense is of all things in the world the most equally distributed; *Premises*: Everybody thinks himself so abundantly provided with it, that even those most difficult to please in all other matters do not commonly desire more of it than they already possess.
Step 2: Not deductively valid
Step 3: Not inductively strong
Step 4: Inductively weak

5. Step 1: *Conclusion*: All absent-minded people are teachers; *Premises*: All philosophers are absent-minded. All philosophers are teachers.
Step 2: Not deductively valid
Step 3: Not inductively strong
Step 4: Deductively invalid

7. Step 1: *Conclusion*: People with high SAT scores—which is very much like IQ tests—also probably have psychic abilities; *Premises*: People with high IQ's also have psychic abilities.
Step 2: Not deductively valid
Step 3: Not inductively strong
Step 4: Inductively weak

8. Step 1: *Conclusion*: There's a conspiracy; *Premises*: If Elvis Presley's name is spelled wrong on his tombstone, there must be some kind of conspiracy surrounding the death of the King. His name is spelled wrong.
Step 2: Deductively valid
Step 3: Does not apply
Step 4: Does not apply

10. Step 1: *Conclusion*: Some people in this neighborhood are bigots; *Premises*: Anyone who is not a bigot will agree that Chris is a good fellow. Some people in this neighborhood think that he's anything but a good fellow.
Step 2: Deductively valid
Step 3: Does not apply
Step 4: Does not apply

11. Step 1: *Conclusion*: In the actual living of life there is no logic; *Premises*: Life is superior to logic.
Step 2: Not deductively valid
Step 3: Not inductively strong
Step 4: Deductively invalid

12. Step 1: *Conclusion*: Someone obviously burglarized the place; *Premises*: A vase was found broken on the floor; some money had been taken out of the safe; and there were strange scratches on the wall.
Step 2: Not deductively valid
Step 3: Inductively strong
Step 4: Does not apply

13. Step 1: *Conclusion*: She's probably guilty; *Premises*: All the evidence in this trial suggests that Lizzy Borden is guilty of murder.
Step 2: Not deductively valid
Step 3: Inductively strong
Step 4: Does not apply

14. Step 1: *Conclusion*: Everything is not all right; *Premises*: If everything was all right, there would be no blood on the floor. Of course, there is plenty of blood on the floor.
Step 2: Deductively valid
Step 3: Does not apply
Step 4: Does not apply

16. Step 1: *Conclusion*: Her training and education must be directed towards that end; *Premises*: From infancy, almost, the average girl is told that marriage is her ultimate goal.
Step 2: Not deductively valid
Step 3: Not inductively strong
Step 4: Inductively weak

17. Step 1: *Conclusion*: Doubtless you have been visited by space aliens; *Premises*: If you have scratches on your body that you can't account for, and you feel that you have been visited by space aliens, then you really have been visited by space aliens. You have such scratches, and you have experienced such feelings.
Step 2: Deductively valid
Step 3: Does not apply
Step 4: Does not apply

18. Step 1: *Conclusion*: War has begun; *Premises*: If bombs are falling on London, war has started. The bombs are falling now.
Step 2: Deductively valid
Step 3: Does not apply
Step 4: Does not apply

Exercise 3-3

1. Strong
2. Valid
4. Valid
5. Strong
6. Valid
7. Valid
9. Strong
10. Weak
11. Valid
12. Valid
13. Strong
15. Weak
16. Valid
17. Valid
19. Weak
20. Valid
21. Strong
22. Invalid

Exercise 3-4

I.

2. Implicit premise: Any runner who is highly motivated will finish the race.

3. Implicit premise: Any movie that grosses over $30 million in the first week at he box office, will win an Oscar.

4. Implicit premise: If the FBI doesn't have a very serious focus on stopping terrorism, another major terrorist attack will happen in this country.

6. Implicit premise: No genuine war can be morally justified.

7. Implicit premise: If the Taliban regime falls, it will be because it persecuted women.

8. Implicit premise: Any Western government that doesn't have the resources to cover the whole world should limit its activities to the Western Hemisphere.

10. Implicit premise: Taslima did not criticize U.S. military action in the Gulf War or in the war in Afghanistan. She must be a hawk.

II.

1. *Added premise*: All the experts agree that any coach who falls asleep during a game is probably not a very good coach.

2. *Added premise*: Nutritionists have found that anyone who eats regularly at McDonald's is likely to gain a few pounds.

4. *Changed premise*: A recent poll shows that 71 percent of the students at Goddard Community College are Democrats.

5. *Added premise*: The stolen books were later found in her purse.

7. *Added premise*: The president needs more money to balance the federal budget.

8. *Added premise*: Li Fong is a student at Boston College.

10. *Added premise*: The typical American diet is excessively high in fat.

Exercise 3-5

2. Valid; *modus ponens*
3. Valid; disjunctive syllogism
4. Invalid; affirming the consequent
5. Invalid; denying the antecedent
7. Invalid; affirming the consequent
8. Invalid; denying the antecedent
10. Valid; *modus tollens*
11. Invalid; affirming the consequent
12. Valid; hypothetical syllogism

Exercise 3-6

1. If the theory of evolution was untrue, biology would make no sense. The theory of evolution is untrue. Therefore, biology makes no sense.

If the theory of evolution was untrue, biology would make no sense. Biology does make sense. Therefore, the theory of evolution is true.

3. If some wars are just, then pacifism is false. Some wars are just. Thus, pacifism is false.

If some wars are just, then pacifism is false. But pacifism is true. Therefore, it's not the case that some wars are just.

4. If the new vaccine prevents the spread of the virus, the researchers who developed the vaccine should get the Nobel prize. It does prevent the spread of the virus. Therefore, the researchers who developed the vaccine should get the Nobel prize.

If the new vaccine prevents the spread of the virus, the researchers who developed the vaccine should get the Nobel prize. The researchers will not get the Nobel prize. Therefore, the new vaccine does not prevent the spread of the virus.

6. If p, then q; p; *therefore, q.*

If p, then q; not-q; *therefore,* not-p.

7. If the glaciers are melting, global warming has increased. The glaciers are melting. Therefore, global warming has increased.

If the glaciers are melting, global warming has increased. Global warming has not increased. Therefore, the glaciers are not melting.

8. If there is such a thing as moral progress—that is, social changes in which we judge states of affairs to be "better" now than before—then the Enlightenment ideal of moral perfection is possible. There is such a thing as progress. Therefore, the Enlightenment ideal of moral perfection is possible.

If there is such a thing as moral progress—that is, social changes in which we judge states of affairs to be "better" now than before—then the Enlightenment ideal of moral perfection is possible. But the Enlightenment ideal of moral perfection is not possible. Therefore, there is no such thing as progress.

10. If my honorable colleague would stop listening to only his own voice for less than sixty seconds, he would doubtless be astonished that there are other minds in the world with other ideas. My honorable colleague will stop listening to only his own voice for less than sixty seconds. Therefore, he will be astonished that there are other minds in the world with other ideas.

If my honorable colleague would stop listening to only his own voice for less than sixty seconds, he would doubtless be astonished that there are other minds in the world with other ideas. He will not be astonished that there are other minds in the world with other ideas. Therefore, he will not stop listening to only his own voice for less than sixty seconds.

Exercise 3-7

4. *Parallel argument*: If Bill Clinton was born in New York, he is an American citizen. He is an American citizen. Therefore, he was born in New York.

If *a*, then *b*.
b.
∴ *a*.

5. *Parallel argument:* If Mickey Mouse was real, he would be famous all over the world. But he's not real. Therefore, he is not famous all over the world.

If *a*, then *b*.
not-*a*.
∴ not-*b*.

7. *Parallel argument:* If George W. Bush lives in Alaska, he lives in North America. He lives in North America. Therefore, he lives in Alaska.

If *a*, then *b*.
b.
∴ *a*.

8. *Parallel argument:* If I'm a kangaroo, I'm warm-blooded. But I'm not a kangaroo. So I'm not warm-blooded.

If *a*, then *b*.
not-*a*.
∴ not-*b*.

11. *Parallel argument:* If Christians worship Satan, they are religious. They are religious; thus, they worship Satan.

If *a*, then *b*.
b.
∴ *a*.

Exercise 3-8

2. (1) If the lights are on, he's home. (2) The lights are on. (3) Therefore, he's home.

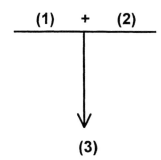

3. (1) It's clear that John stole the money. (2) His fingerprints were found all over the place. (3) Fingerprint evidence is a very reliable kind of evidence that was vouched for by the police.

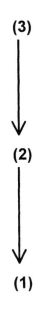

5. (1) If it had rained last night, the streets would be wet. (2) And the streets are wet. (3) Therefore, it rained last night. (4) And that means it was impossible to do any stargazing last night.

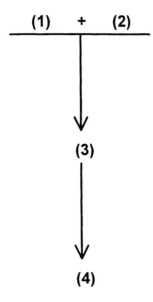

6. (1) If the experiment had succeeded, there would have been a massive explosion. (2) And there was such an explosion. (3) So we have a success. (4) If we have a success, we will win the Nobel prize. (5) Therefore, we will win the Nobel prize.

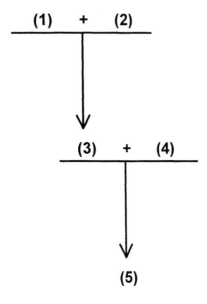

7. (1) If the dog bit the mail carrier, there would have been a scar on her leg. (2) And some witnesses said that they saw the scar. (3) But in any case, the mail carrier didn't deny having a scar. (4) So the dog probably bit the mail carrier. (5) And if that's the case, the carrier has grounds for a law suit. (6)Ergo, she has grounds for a law suit.

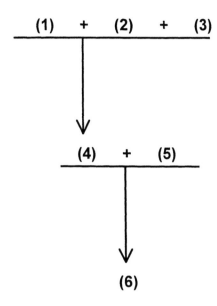

Exercise 3-9

1. (1) I shouldn't take physics this semester. (2) My course load is already too heavy. (3) There's no room for the course in my schedule. (4) And I don't like physics.

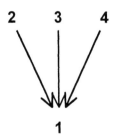

2. (1) The president is soft on the environment. (2) He has weakened clean-air regulations (3) and lifted restrictions on logging in the West.

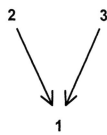

3. (1) Congressman Porkbarrel is either dishonest or incompetent. (2) He's not incompetent, though, because he's expert at getting self-serving legislation through Congress. (3) I guess he's just dishonest.

4. (1) If an individual in a coma is no longer a person, then giving him a drug to kill him is not murder. (2) Such an individual is in fact not a person. (3) Therefore, giving him the drug is not murder.

5. (1) The City Council deserves the gratitude of all New Yorkers for introducing a bill to ban the use of cell phones in places of public performance…(2) These rules may be hard to enforce, but so are bans on littering, auto horn honking and other quality-of-life offenses. (3) By changing the law, the city will send a clear message that cell phone abuse is not just an etiquette issue but robs audience members of their right to enjoy the performance they paid for.

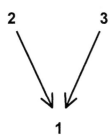

7. (1) If you gain too much weight, your blood pressure will increase. (2) If your blood pressure increases, your risk of stroke or heart attack rises. (3) Therefore, gaining too much weight can increase your risk of stroke and heart attack.

8. (1) Grow accustomed to the belief that death is nothing to us, (2) since every good and evil lie in sensation. (3) However, death is the deprivation of sensation. (4) Therefore…death is nothing to us.

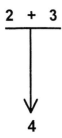

9. (1) A cause-and-effect relationship is drawn [by those opposed to pornography] between men viewing pornography and men attacking women, especially in the form of rape. (2) But studies and experts disagree as to whether any relationship exists between pornography and violence, between images and behavior. (3) Even the pro-censorship Meese Commission Report admitted that the data connecting pornography to violence was unreliable. *Implied*: (4) Therefore, the alleged cause-and-effect relationship is dubious.

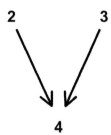

11. (1) If Li Yang gets a high score on her test, she will have a perfect grade point average. (2) If she gets a low score, she will drop out of school. (3) She will get a high score on the test, (4) so she will have a perfect grade point average.

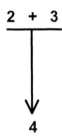

12. (1) Most atheists are liberals, and (2) George is an atheist. Therefore, (3) George is probably a liberal. (4) Therefore George is probably in favor of increased welfare benefits (5) because most liberals are in favor of increased welfare benefits.

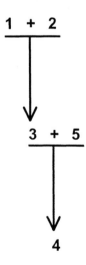

13. (1) Bill is a student at Yale. (2) No student at Yale has won the Nobel prize. (3) Therefore, Bill has not won the Nobel prize.

14. (1) An international agreement proscribes the use of gas and (2) so germ warfare must be developed.

15. (1) The only valid reasons for dishonorably discharging someone from the Army are health problems and violations of Army regulations. (2) So if Amal says that he was dishonorably discharged for simply being gay, he is lying or is mistaken. (3) He is not lying. (4) So he is mistaken.

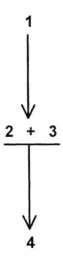

16. (1) It is clear that archaeologists have not yet come to terms with dowsing [the alleged ability to detect underground water or treasure by paranormal means]. (2) Where it has been the subject of tests, the tests have been so poorly designed and executed that any conclusion whatsoever could have been drawn from them. (3) The fact that such tests are usually carried out only by researchers with a prior positive view of dowsing means that the conclusions will likely also be positive. (4) The normal processes of peer review and scholarly discussion have also failed to uncover the lack of properly controlled test conditions in such studies as those of Bailey et al and Locock, causing a generation of students and general readers in the United Kingdom, at least, to remain under the impression that the reality of archaeological dowsing had been all but confirmed by science.

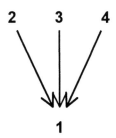

18. (1) Some say that those without strong religious beliefs—nonbelievers in one form or another—cannot be moral. (2) But millions upon millions of people have been nonbelievers or nontheists and yet have produced some of the most noble and most morally principled civilizations in history. (3) Consider the Buddhists of Asia and the Confucianists of China. (4) Consider also the great secular philosophers from the ancient Greeks to the likes of Bertrand Russell and John Searle of the twentieth century. (5) *Implied*: It's not true that those without strong religious beliefs cannot be moral.

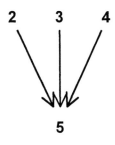

19. (1) Either Maggie, Jose, or Ling broke the window. (2) Jose couldn't have done it because he was studying in his room and was observed the whole time. (3) Maggie couldn't have done it because she was out of town at the time and has witnesses to prove it. (4) So the thief had to be Ling.

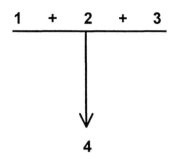

21. (1) The Golden Gate bridge will probably be attacked by terrorists within the next two years. (2) The latest intelligence reports from the Justice Department confirm this prediction. (3) Plus terrorists have already stated publicly that they intend to destroy various symbolic structures or monuments in the United States, including Mount Rushmore and the Golden Gate.

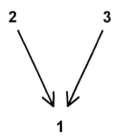

22. (1) We shouldn't pay Edward an allowance (2) because he never does any work around the house, and (3) he will probably just waste the money because (4) he has no conception of the value of anything.

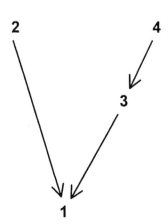

Exercise 3-10

2. *Conclusion*: (1) When [Gillespie] refers to [President Bush] as "the millionaire president who waited out the Vietnam War in the Texas Air National Guard," it reminds me of the garbage rhetoric that I might see if I were reading Ted Rall, or Susan Sontag, or one of the other hate-mongering, America-bashing, leftist whiners. [*Paraphrase*: Gillespie's rhetoric is inappropriate.] *Premises*: (2) That kind of ad hominem attack [is] disrespectful to a man who is doing a damned good job as commander-in-chief. (3) [The rhetoric] it detracts from the whole point of the article.

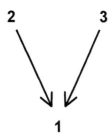

3. *Conclusion*: (1) Therefore some intelligent being exists by whom all natural things are directed to their end; and this being we call God. *Premises*: (2) We see that things which lack knowledge, such as natural bodies, act for an end, and this is evident from their acting always, or nearly always, in the same way, so as to obtain the best result. (3) Hence it is plain that they achieve their end, not fortuitously, but designedly. (4) Now whatever lacks knowledge cannot move towards an end, unless it be directed by some being endowed with knowledge and intelligence; as the arrow is directed by the archer.

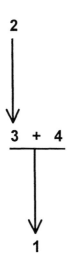

4. *Conclusion*: (1) [The] position is certainly untenable. *Premises*: (2) The first thing that must occur to anyone studying moral subjectivism [the view that the rightness or wrongness of an action depends on the beliefs of an individual or group] seriously is that the view allows the possibility that an action can be both right and not right, or wrong and not wrong, etc. (3) This possibility exists because, as we have seen, the subjectivist claims that the moral character of an action is determined by individual subjective states; and these states can vary from person to person, even when directed toward the same action on the same occasion. (4) Hence one and the same action can evidently be determined to have—simultaneously—radically different moral characters…

3

2

4

1

5. *Conclusion*: (1) I submit that the dismissal was proper and ethical considering the community stature and function of priests and the benefits that accrue to society in the aftermath of the decision. *Premises*: Let's consider community stature first. The community stature of priests must always be taken into account in these abuse cases. (2) A priest is not just anybody; he performs a special role in society—namely, to provide spiritual guidance and to remind people that there is both a moral order and a divine order in the world. The priest's role is special because it helps to underpin and secure society itself. (3) Anything that could undermine this role must be neutralized as soon a possible. (4) Among those things that can weaken the priestly role are publicity, public debate, and legal actions. Abuse cases are better handled in private by those who are keenly aware of the importance of a positive public image of priests. And what of the benefits of curtailing the legal proceedings? (5) The benefits to society of dismissing the legal case outweigh all the alleged disadvantages of continuing with public hearings. (6) The primary benefit is the continued nurturing of the community's faith, without which the community would cease to function effectively.

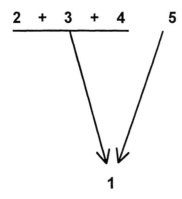

TEST BANK

Multiple Choice
(Correct answers are marked with an asterisk.)

1. A deductive argument is intended to provide…
        a. Probable support for its conclusion
        b. Persuasive support for its conclusion
        * c. Logically conclusive support for its conclusion
        d. Tentative support for its conclusion

2. A deductive argument that succeeds in providing logically conclusive support is said to be…
        a. Strong
        b. Probabilistic
        c. Invalid
        * d. Valid

3. An inductive argument is intended to provide...
   a. Valid support for its conclusion
   * b. Probable support for its conclusion
   c. Weak support for its conclusion
   d. Truth-preserving support for its conclusion

4. An inductive argument that succeeds in providing probable support for its conclusion is said to be
   * a. Strong
   b. Valid
   c. Invalid
   d. Weak

5. A deductively valid argument that has true premises is said to be...
   a. Strong
   * b. Sound
   c. Cogent
   d. Probable

6. A deductively valid argument CANNOT have...
   * a. True premises and false conclusion
   b. False premises and false conclusion
   c. False premises and true conclusion
   d. True premises and true conclusion

7. An inductively strong argument with true premises is said to be...
   a. Sound
   b. Valid
   c. Invalid
   * d. Cogent

8. Terms that signal a deductive argument include...
   a. "Probably," "chances are," and "likely"
   b. "Formally," "broadly," and "odds are"
   c. "It is plausible that," "almost," and "finally"
   *d. "Necessarily, " "it follows that," and "absolutely"

9. The first step in uncovering implicit premises is to search for a credible premise that would make the argument ...
   a. Strong
   b. Complete
   * c. Valid
   d. Plausible

10. The argument pattern known as *modus ponens* is …
    a. Invalid
    b. Strong
    * c. Valid
    d. Weak

True/False
(Correct answers marked with an asterisk.)

1. The argument form *modus tollens* has this form: If *p*, then *q*; Not-*q*; Therefore not-*p*.
    * a. True
    b. False

2. The argument form known as hypothetical syllogisms is always invalid.
    a. True
    * b. False

3. The argument form known as denying the antecedent is always valid.
    a. True
    *b. False

4. Deductively valid arguments are truth-preserving.
    * a. True
    b. False

5. A deductively valid argument is such that if its premises are true, its conclusion must be false.
    a. True
    * b. False

6. An inductive argument that fails to provide probable support for its conclusion is said to be strong.
    a. True
    *b. False

7. If a deductively valid argument has a false conclusion, you can infer that at least one of the premises is false.
    * a. True
    b. False

8. The second part of a conditional statement is known as the consequent.
    * a. True
    b. False

9. The argument form known as affirming the consequent is valid.
    a. True
    * b. False

10. The counterexample method is used to determine whether an argument is valid or invalid.
   * a. True
   b. False

Short Answer/Short Essay

1. What is the procedure for determining whether an argument is deductive or inductive, valid or invalid, and strong or weak?

2. According to the text, what is the difference between persuading and reasoning?

3. What does it mean for an argument to be valid or invalid?

4. What does it mean for an argument to be strong or weak?

5. What are two major differences between the argument form known as *modus tollens* and denying the antecedent?

6. What is the counterexample method and how is it applied to arguments?

7. According to the text, what steps are involved in diagramming an argument?

8. According to the text, what are the four basic steps in assessing a long argument?

9. In what way are deductively valid arguments truth-preserving?

10. What is the difference between a deductive argument's truth and its validity? How are these two related?

Chapter 4
Reasons for Belief and Doubt

This chapter focuses on evaluating the reliability of claims that are generally not supported by argument or evidence—probably the kind of claims that students encounter most. This category encompasses all manner of unsupported statements, including those that come from our own personal experience and reflection, those that hit us from all sides in our daily lives (and are often conflicting), those that issue from experts, and those that arise from the news media.

This material is very straightforward, but it's likely to catch many students off guard because they probably haven't thought much about what's reasonable or unreasonable to believe regarding all the claims they encounter. They need to both understand the principles involved and be able to apply them in appropriate circumstances. So substantial class time and practice may be necessary to ensure that the material sinks in.

Perhaps the most useful approach is to present the students with a list of claims (such as those in Exercises 4-2 and 4-3) and ask them how much credence they would give each one and why, taking into account the principles they've learned. Whether done in class or out, such exercises encourage students to think about the *reasons* for their degree of belief or disbelief in various claims.

CHAPTER SUMMARY

Many times we need to be able to evaluate an unsupported claim—a claim that isn't backed by an argument. There are several critical thinking principles that can help us do this. An important one is: *If a claim conflicts with other claims we have good reason to accept, we have good grounds for doubting it.* Sometimes the conflict is between a claim and your background information. Background information is the large collection of very well supported beliefs that we rely on to inform our actions and choices. The relevant principle then is: *If a claim conflicts with our background information, we have good reason to doubt the claim.*

It's not reasonable to accept a claim if there is good reason to doubt it. In the case of claims that we can neither accept nor reject outright: *We should proportion our belief to the evidence.*

An expert is someone who is more knowledgeable in a particular subject area than most others are. The important principle here is: *If a claim conflicts with expert opinion, we have good reason to doubt it.* We must couple this principle with another one: *When the experts disagree about a claim, we have good reason to doubt it.* When we rely on bogus expert opinion, we commit the fallacy known as the appeal to authority.

Many claims are based on nothing more than personal experience, ours or someone else's. We can trust our personal experience—to a point. The guiding principle is: *It's reasonable to accept the evidence provided by personal experience only if there's no reason to doubt it.* Some common factors that can raise such doubts are impairment (stress, injury, distraction, emotional upset, and the like), expectation, and our limited abilities in judging probabilities.

Some of the common mistakes we make in evaluating claims is resisting contrary evidence, looking for confirming evidence, and preferring available evidence. To counteract these tendencies, we need to take deliberate steps to critically examine even our most cherished claims, search for disconfirming evidence as well as confirming, and look beyond evidence that is merely the most striking or memorable.

Many of the unsupported claims we encounter are in news reports. Reporters, editors, and producers are under many pressures that can lead to biased or misleading reporting. The biggest factor is money—the drive for profits in news organizations, especially those owned by larger corporations or conglomerates. Reporters themselves may introduce inaccuracies, biases, and personal opinions. And the people who produce the news may decide not to cover certain stories (or aspects of stories), which can sometimes provide a skewed or erroneous picture of an issue or event.

The best defense against being misled by news reports is a reasonable skepticism and a critical approach that involves, among other things, looking for slanting, examining sources, checking for missing facts, and being on the lookout for false emphasis.

EXERCISES NOT ANSWERED IN THE TEXT

Exercise 4-1

1. The large collection of very well supported beliefs that we all rely on to inform our actions and choices.
2. If a claim conflicts with other claims we have good reason to accept, we have good grounds for doubting it.
3. We should doubt any claim that conflicts with our background information, and we should assign a low probability to any claim that conflicts with a great deal of our background information.
5. Someone who is more knowledgeable in a particular subject area or field than most others are.
6. If a claim conflicts with expert opinion, we have good reason to doubt it.
7. When the experts disagree about a claim, we have good reason to doubt it.
8. The fallacy of relying on the opinion of someone deemed to be an expert who in fact is *not* an expert.
9. (1) Education and training from reputable institutions or programs in the relevant field, and (2) experience in making reliable judgments in the field.
11. We often suspect bias when an expert is being paid by special-interest groups or companies to render an opinion, when the expert expresses very strong belief in a claim even though there is no evidence to support it, or when the expert stands to gain financially from the actions or policies that he or she supports.
12. It's reasonable to accept the evidence provided by personal experience only if there's no good reason to doubt it.
13. Any two: impairment, expectation, or innumeracy
14. The error of thinking that previous events can affect the probabilities in the random event at hand.
15. Possible answer: People may deny the evidence, ignore it, or reinterpret it.
16. The tendency to seek out or use only confirming evidence.
18. Relying on evidence not because it's trustworthy but because it's memorable or striking.

19. If we're in the habit of basing our judgments on evidence that's merely psychologically available, we will frequently commit the error known as hasty generalization—drawing a conclusion about a whole group based on an inadequate sample of the group.

20. The foremost factor is money—the need for news media to make a profit, pay salaries, and please stockholders.

21. Possible answer: (1) Considering whether the report conflicts with what you have good reason to believe, (2) looking for reporter slanting, and (3) checking for missing information.

Exercise 4-2

1. Reject; the claim conflicts with background information and reliable scientific claims about psychic phenomena.

2. Reject; the claim conflicts with background information (the scientific fact that the biological life span of humans is a maximum of 120 years).

3. Proportion belief to the evidence; the claim is probably false (because nowadays leprosy can be cured, and because the disease is virtually unheard of in the United States).

5. Reject; the claim conflicts with background information (including especially the known scarcity of pygmy hippos).

7. Proportion belief to the evidence; the claim is probably false (because such collusion would be easily detected and because there seems to be no plausible motive for why the United States would act against French Canadians).

8. Proportion belief to the evidence; the claim is very likely to be false (because of the very low probability of a nonexpert accurately predicting stock prices and recessions).

9. Proportion belief to the evidence; the claim is probably false (because of the low probability of shark attacks in general and because the past incidence of such a strange attack seems to be zero).

11. Reject; the claim conflicts with background information (the lack of evidence for any psychic or occult phenomena ever occurring and the failure of scientific studies to support the idea of psychic healing).

12. Accept; in general, such reports from the NIH are very reliable.

13. Reject; the claim conflicts with background information (the extreme scarcity of albino alligators and the fact that no giant alligators have every been found in the sewers of New York, despite urban legends to the contrary).

14. Reject; the claim conflicts with background information (the existence of space aliens and the lack of evidence for crop circles being made by anyone other than humans).

15. Accept; existing evidence strongly suggests that all crop circles are made by humans.

16. Proportion belief to the evidence; the claim is very likely to be false (because dramatically lowering taxes and greatly increasing spending usually causes deficits).

18. Proportion belief to the evidence; depending on how "viable" is defined, the claim seems more likely to be false than true (because some modern democracies do in fact seem viable).

19. Reject; the claim conflicts with background information (basic gastroenterological facts).

20. Accept; New York state drivers can see for themselves that the claim is true.

Exercise 4-3

These unanswered exercises (1, 2, 4, 5, 6, 7, 9, 10) are best left to students to answer since the point is to get them to evaluate their own opinions.

Exercise 4-4

1. The story does not simply report the facts regarding "time cheating" by city construction employees. It takes a strong stance against the employees, adopting a tone of moral indignation about their alleged activities and, contrary to the usual news practice, assuming that the allegations are justified. This tone is reinforced, and the employees' infractions are made to seem all the worse, by the claim in the first paragraph that the employees committed crimes when they could have been engaged in acceptable behavior such as "spending their days at the gym, shopping or moonlighting."
2. Loaded language is used throughout the story to bias the reader against the employees—for example, "*Brazen* Department of Education construction employees..."; "employees *ripped off the city*..."; "The *slackers* will soon find themselves..."; and "...did not release the names of the *slackers*."
3. Apparently, the main source for this story seems to be one person—Schools Investigator Richard Condon—though there is a reference to unnamed "authorities."

TEST BANK

Multiple Choice
(Correct answers are marked with an asterisk.)

1. If a claim conflicts with other claims we have good reason to accept, we have good grounds for...
    a. Believing it
    b. Rejecting it
    c. Accepting it
    * d. Doubting it

2. Your background information consists of ...
    a. Beliefs that are certain
    b. Both well supported and obviously false beliefs
    c. Numerous valid arguments
    * d. Very well supported beliefs

3. If a claim conflicts with our background information, we have good reason to...
    a. Accept it
    * b. Doubt it
    c. Reject it
    d. Replace it

4. When a claim is neither worthy of outright rejection nor deserving of complete acceptance, we should...

    * a. Proportion our belief to the evidence
    b. Proportion our belief to background information
    c. Tentatively accept it
    d. Tentatively reject it

5. It's not reasonable to believe a claim when...

    a. The claim is criticized
    b. Most people reject it
    * c. There is no good reason for doing so
    d. There is no good reason for examining it

6. We are often justified in believing a claim because...

    a. Most people believe it
    b. Experts disagree about it
    c. Experts have not accepted it
    * d. It comes from experts

7. When experts disagree about a claim, we have good reason to...

    a. Reject it
    b. Believe it
    * c. Doubt it
    d. Dismiss it

8. The two most revealing indicators of an expert's reliability are...

    a. Education and experience in making reliable judgments
    b. Education and lack of conflicts of interest
    c. Reputation and training
    *d. Reputation among peers and professional accomplishments

9. It's reasonable to accept the evidence provided by personal experience only if...

    a. It is backed by scientific evidence
    * b. There's no good reason to doubt it
    c. We are infallible
    d. It is corroborated by other people

10. Research shows that our perception and memory are...

    a. Destructive
    b. Recording devices
    c. Rarely wrong
    * d. Constructive

True/False
(Correct answers marked with an asterisk.)

1. What we perceive and remember is to some degree fabricated by our minds.
   * a. True
   b. False

2. In the phenomenon known as pareidolia, we may see and hear exactly what we expect to hear.
   * a. True
   b. False

3. The idea that future events can affect the past is known as the gambler's fallacy.
   a. True
   *b. False

4. Confirmation bias does not affect scientists.
   a. True
   * b. False

5. Relying on the best possible evidence when evaluating claims is known as the availability error.
   a. True
   * b. False

6. Most reporters are investigative journalists.
   a. True
   *b. False

7. It's not reasonable to believe a claim when there is no good reason for doing so.
   * a. True
   b. False

8. Experts in one field can usually make trustworthy claims regarding other fields.
   a. True
   * b. False

9. We may reasonably suspect that an expert is biased when he or she expresses strong belief in a claim that has no supporting evidence.
   * a. True
   b. False

10. Humans are not very good at estimating probabilities.
   * a. True
   b. False

Short Answer/Short Essay

1. What principle should guide us in assessing the reliability of personal experience?

2. Why are experts more likely to be right than nonexperts?

3. What should we do when a claim is in dispute among experts? ?

4. Are doctors experts in determining whether a particular treatment is safe and effective? Why or why not?

5. Is it reasonable to regard a nonexpert as an expert? Why or why not?

6. What is confirmation bias? How does it affect our thinking?

7. What is the availability error? How does it affect our thinking?

8. According to the text, why is eyewitness testimony often suspect? What factors can undermine the reliability of eyewitness testimony?

9. According to the text, why is it that coincidences *must* occur?

10. How can confirmation bias affect people's thinking? According to the text, how can we counteract our tendency toward confirmation bias?

Chapter 5
Faulty Reasoning

A chapter on informal fallacies could easily become encyclopedic, listing dozens of them, categorized in all sorts of ways. This chapter doesn't take that tack. The premise behind it is that it's better to cover a smaller number of fallacies in some depth than to try to say a little something about dozens of them. So here are fifteen informal fallacies (with some subtypes), covered in some detail and chosen because they seem, on an educated guess, more likely than others to be encountered by students and to cause them trouble.

This chapter's highest objective is to get students to spot fallacies in the rough and to avoid being taken in by them. A secondary objective is for students to be able to identify fallacies by name—but this second objective is just a convenient way to get a handle on the first. So the exercises, field problems, and writing assignments are mostly identification drills, with some of them asking students to go a few steps further and identify fallacies in their classmates' papers and to rewrite fallacy-laden passages.

Note that the material here is quite modular. It lends itself to being profitably taken up at any point in the course or in any sequence of chapters.

CHAPTER SUMMARY

Certain types of defective arguments that occur frequently are known as fallacies. Fallacies are often psychologically persuasive but logically flawed. We can divide fallacies into two broad categories: (1) those that have *irrelevant* premises and (2) those that have *unacceptable* premises.

Fallacies with irrelevant premises include the **Genetic Fallacy** (arguing that a claim is true or false solely because of its origin), **Composition** (arguing that what is true of the parts must be true of the whole), **Division** (arguing that what is true of the whole must be true of the parts, or that what is true of a group is true of individuals in the group), **Appeal to the Person** (rejecting a claim by criticizing the person who makes it rather than the claim itself), **Equivocation** (the use of a word in two different senses in an argument), **Appeal to the Masses** (arguing that a claim must be true merely because a substantial number of people believe it), **Appeal to Ignorance** (arguing that a lack of evidence proves something), **Appeal to Tradition** (arguing that a claim must be true or good just because it's part of a tradition), **Appeal to Emotion** (the use of emotions as premises in an argument), **Red Herring** (the deliberate raising of an irrelevant issue during an argument), and **Straw Man** (the distorting, weakening, or oversimplifying of someone's position so it can be more easily attacked or refuted).

Fallacies with unacceptable premises include **Begging the Question** (the attempt to establish the conclusion of an argument by using that conclusion as a premise), **Slippery Slope** (arguing, without good reasons, that taking a particular step will inevitably lead to a further, undesirable step or steps), **Hasty Generalization** (the drawing of a conclusion about a group based on an inadequate sample of the group), and **Faulty Analogy** (an argument in which the things being compared are not sufficiently similar in relevant ways).

EXERCISES NOT ANSWERED IN THE TEXT

Exercise 5-1

1. Those that have *irrelevant* premises and those that have *unacceptable* premises.
2. The fallacy of arguing that a claim is true or false solely because of its origin.
3. Yes
5. Arguing that what is true of the whole must be true of the parts, and arguing that what is true of a group is true of individuals in the group.
6. Appeals to the person are fallacious because they attempt to discredit a claim by appealing to something that's almost always irrelevant to it: a person's character, motives, or personal circumstances.
7. *Tu quoque*
8. The fallacy of insisting that someone has no regard for the truth or has nonrational motives for espousing a claim and therefore nothing that he or she says should be believed, including the claim in question.
9. The fallacy of using a word in two different senses in an argument.
11. The fallacy of arguing that a claim must be true just because it's part of a tradition.
12. One form says that a claim must be true because it hasn't been shown to be false, and another form says that a claim must be false because it hasn't been proved to be true.
13. In general, if the claimant makes an unsupported positive claim, he or she must provide evidence for it if the claim is to be accepted. If you doubt the claim, you are under no obligation to prove it wrong. You need not—and should not—accept it without good reasons (which the claimant should provide). Of course, you also should not reject the claim without good reasons. If the claimant does provide you with reasons for accepting the claim, you can either accept them or reject them. If you reject them, you are obligated to explain the reasons for your rejection.
14. The use of nonargumentative, emotive words and phrases to persuade or influence an audience.
16. The deliberate raising of an irrelevant issue during an argument.
17. Typically, someone using the straw man fallacy reinterprets claim X so that it becomes the weak or absurd claim Y, then attacks claim Y, concluding that X is unfounded.
18. The fallacy of attempting to establish the conclusion of an argument by using that conclusion as a premise.
20. The weight of evidence or argument required by one side in a debate or disagreement.
21. The fallacy of arguing, without good reasons, that taking a particular step will inevitably lead to further, undesirable steps.

Exercise 5-2

2. Appeal to the masses
3. Appeal to the person (*tu quoque*)
4. The statement is ambiguous, so it could contain an appeal to the person (maybe *tu quoque*) or possibly the genetic fallacy.
6. Straw man
7. Appeal to tradition
8. Division

9. Appeal to the masses
11. Red herring
12. Appeal to tradition
13. Genetic fallacy
15. Appeal to emotion
16. Appeal to ignorance
17. Appeal to the person (both *tu quoque* and name-calling))
18. Appeal to the masses
20. Appeal to ignorance
21. Appeal to emotion and possibly red herring
22. Equivocation
23. Composition

Exercise 5-3

1. Begging the question
2. Slippery slope
3. Begging the question
5. False dilemma
7. Hasty generalization
8. No fallacy
9. Faulty analogy

Exercise 5-4

1. The federal budget deficit will destroy the economy. The problem is overspending. Those fat cats in the U.S. Senate have voted themselves a raise, and they're already being paid way too much for the lousy job they're doing. It's overspending like this that causes the deficit, bankrupting the government. And a bankrupt government will make the economy implode.
2. Everybody knows that *Shane* is the best western ever made. Millions of *Shane* fans can't be wrong.
4. Vampires—the blood-sucking phantoms of folklore—are real. And there can be no greater proof of their existence than the failure of science to prove that they are actual. If there really were no vampires, science would have proved their nonexistence by now.
5. People seem completely unaware that Internet pornography can destroy this country. But it's a matter of simple logic. There is no doubt that Internet porn promotes illicit sex—sex that's neither normal nor moral. Once people get involved in illicit sex, they find in much, much easier to allow illicit behavior in other areas of their life. They find it far easier to lie, cheat, steal, and commit violent acts. Immorality and illegality become common. And as every historian knows, when these things become common, society self-destructs.
7. Iran is rapidly developing nuclear weapons. When the Iranians finally possess these weapons, they will—either overtly or implicitly—threaten the world with them. A nuclear catastrophe will be inevitable. And there seems to be no way short of military action to prevent it. The United States therefore has only two choices: It can sit back and allow this terrifying state of affairs to happen, or it can attack Iran and destroy the weapons. Allowing nuclear holocaust to happen is not an option. Thus, the United States must attack Iran.

8. That economics seminar is absolutely the worst course offered at the university. I took that course, and so did two of my friends. And we all concluded that the course was absolutely the most dreadful one here.

9. Pope John Paul II is a moral giant. He has traveled all over the world, promoting a message of peace and goodness. When he went to Africa, he was surrounded by crippled children eager to touch him and speak with him. With a tear in his eye, he welcomed all of them and touched all of them. Many of those children smiled, probably for the first time in their lives.

10. The Nigerian court was right to sentence that woman to be stoned to death for adultery. Everybody knows that the court's action was right.

12. All efforts should be made to ban trade in exotic pets such as tigers. The opposite view—that it's not the case that all such efforts should be made to ban trade in exotic pets—is clearly false because it comes straight from the Republican party, which is notoriously anti-environment.

TEST BANK

Multiple Choice
(Correct answers are marked with an asterisk.)

1. Fallacies are often beguiling because they are psychologically persuasive yet…
    a. Psychologically sound
    b. Morally right
    c. Logically correct
    * d. Logically inadequate

2. The genetic fallacy is arguing that a claim is true or false solely because of its…
    a. Premises
    * b. Origin
    c. Analogies
    d. Form

3. The fallacy of arguing that what is true of the parts must be true of the whole is called…
    a. Division
    * b. Composition
    c. Equivocation
    d. Faulty analogy

4. The fallacy of rejecting a claim by criticizing the person who makes it rather than the claim itself is known as. …
    * a. Appeal to the person
    b. Appeal to emotion
    c. Appeal to the masses
    d. Appeal to tradition

5. A type of *ad hominem* fallacy that argues that a claim must be true (or false) just because the claimant is hypocritical is called…
    a. Personal attack
    * b. *Tu quoque*
    c. Poisoning the well
    d. Equivocation

6. The fallacy of arguing that a claim must be true merely because a substantial number of people believe it is known as…
    a. Appeal to emotion
    b. Appeal to ignorance
    c. Appeal to tradition
    * d. Appeal to the masses

7. Usually the burden of proof rests on the side that…
    a. Is winning
    b. Makes a negative claim
    c. Tries to prove a negative
    * d. Makes a positive claim

8. The fallacy of deliberately raising an irrelevant issue during an argument is called…
    * a. Red herring
    b. Appeal to ignorance
    c. Straw man
    d. Composition

9. The fallacy sometimes referred to as arguing in a circle is the fallacy of …
    a. False dilemma
    b. Slippery slope
    * c. Begging the question
    d. Hasty generalization

10. Slippery slope is a fallacy of …
    a. Irrelevant premises
    * b. Unacceptable premises
    c. Unacceptable dilemmas
    d. Irrelevant conclusions

True/False
(Correct answers marked with an asterisk.)

1. Whether people are hypocritical regarding their claims is directly related to the truth of those claims.
    a. True
    * b. False

2. Claims should be regarded as true if they are believed by many people.
    a. True
    * b. False

3. A scientific claim must be true if it hasn't been shown to be false.
    a. True
    *b. False

4. If we could prove something with a lack of evidence, we could prove almost anything.
    * a. True
    b. False

5. Good writers never combine arguments with appeals to emotion.
    a. True
    * b. False

6. The following argument pattern is an example of begging the question: Reinterpret claim X so that it becomes the weak or absurd claim Y; attack claim Y; conclude that X is unfounded.
    a. True
    *b. False

7. The attempt to establish the conclusion of an argument by using that conclusion as a premise is known as slippery slope.
    a. True
    * b. False

8. Slippery slope arguments are fallacious because they offer no good reasons for believing that the sequence of steps referred to will happen as predicted.
    * a. True
    b. False

9. The following argument is an example of equivocation: The political action committee is very prestigious in Washington; we can expect then that each of its soldiers is very prestigious in Washington.
    a. True
    * b. False

10. The fact that someone has dubious reasons for making a claim shows that the claim is false.
    a. True
    * b. False

Short Answer/Short Essay

1. According to the text, what are the two main categories of fallacies?

2. How is the genetic fallacy used to persuade someone that a claim is true?

3. Why are appeals to the person fallacious?

4. What is the fallacy of equivocation and how can it be used to persuade an audience that a conclusion is true?

5. Why is an appeal to the masses fallacious?

6. What is the relationship between appeals to ignorance and the burden of proof?

7. Why is asking someone to prove a universal negative unreasonable?

8. What is the fallacy of red herring and how is it used to persuade people to accept a claim?

9. What is the basic pattern of a straw man argument? How are straw man arguments sometimes used in debates over church-state separation?

10. According to the text, why are people often taken in by false dilemmas? What question should people ask to avoid falling into these traps?

Chapter 6
Deductive Reasoning: Propositional Logic

This chapter is straightforward enough to follow immediately after the preliminaries of Chapter 3, or even Chapter 2. Regardless of what students may think when they first lay eyes on this chapter (replete as it is with truth tables and scary algebra-type symbols), they *can* "get" this stuff if they give it half a chance. This chapter was developed with the idea that students will probably be intimidated by it right off and may wonder why they should bother. The first few pages try to address these concerns, but probably the best cure for this reluctance is for students to dive in, do the exercises, and make sure they fully understand the material at hand before moving on to the next section. The material is progressive and laid out as clearly as possible without oversimplifying. After completing the first few sets of exercises, most students will probably leave their fears behind and might even enjoy exercises that require unambiguous answers and relatively simple skills.

CHAPTER SUMMARY

In propositional logic we use symbols to stand for the relationships between statements—that is, to indicate the form of an argument. These relationships are made possible by logical connectives such as conjunction (and), disjunction (or), negation (not), and conditional (If…then…). Connectives are used in compound statements, each of which is composed of at least two simple statements. A simple statement is a sentence that can be either true or false.

To indicate the possible truth values of statements and arguments, we can construct truth tables, a graphic way of displaying all the truth value possibilities. A conjunction is false if at least one of its statement components (conjuncts) is false. A disjunction is still true even if one of its component statements (disjuncts) is false. A negation is the denial of a statement. The negation of any statement changes the statement's truth value to its contradictory (false to true, and true to false). A conditional statement is false in only one situation—when the antecedent is true and the consequent is false.

The use of truth tables to determine the validity of an argument is based on the fact that it's impossible for a valid argument to have true premises and a false conclusion. A basic truth table consists of two or more guide columns listing all the truth value possibilities, followed by a column for each premise and the conclusion. We can add other columns to help us determine the truth values of components of the argument.

Some arguments are complex when variables and connectives are combined into larger compounds and when the number of variables increases. To prevent confusion, we can use parentheses in symbolized arguments to show how statement or premise components go together.

You can check the validity of arguments not only with truth tables but also with the short method. In this procedure we try to discover if there is a way to make the conclusion false and the premises true by assigning various truth values to the argument's components.

EXERCISES NOT ANSWERED IN THE TEXT

Exercise 6-1

2. Disjunction; components: I walk home; I drive Ralph's car; **v**
3. Conditional; components: Yankees win; they will be in the world series; →
4. Negation; component: Yankees won; ~
6. Disjunction; components: The newspaper ad was misleading; it was meant as a joke; **v**
8. Conjunction; components: He supported the revolution; he was arrested without being charged; **&**

Exercise 6-2

2. $p \lor q$
3. $\sim a$
5. $\sim c$
6. $x \to y$
7. $\sim q \to p$
9. $j \mathbin{\&} k$
10. $\sim b$
11. $y \to x$
12. $p \lor q$
13. $d \to e$
15. $s \lor t$
16. $p \mathbin{\&} q$

Exercise 6-3

1. T
3. T
4. F
5. T
7. T
9. T
10. T

Exercise 6-4

1. F
3. F
4. T
6. T
7. T
8. T
9. F

Exercise 6-5

1. Alligators are reptiles, and puppies are mammals.
3. If the cat was on the mat, then Quentin was home.
4. Either babies can't fly, or cats can fly.
6. Alice is here, and Quentin is not here.
7. Either the bakery is open, or the pub is not open.
8. Alice sang, and Carl played the piano.
9. If Bob drove home, then Cathy will not leave.

Exercise 6-6

1. $p \rightarrow q$
3. $p \vee q$
4. $\sim p$ & $\sim q$
6. $p \rightarrow q$
7. p & $\sim q$
8. $\sim p$ & $\sim q$
10. p & $\sim q$

Exercise 6-7

1. $p \vee q$

p	q	p ∨ q
T	T	T
T	F	T
F	T	T
F	F	F

3. $\sim p$ & $\sim q$

p	q	~ p	~ q	~ p & ~ q
T	T	F	F	F
T	F	F	T	F
F	T	T	F	F
F	F	T	T	T

4. $p \rightarrow q$

p	q	p → q
T	T	T
T	F	F
F	T	T
F	F	T

5. $p \rightarrow q$

p	q	$p \rightarrow q$
T	T	T
T	F	F
F	T	T
F	F	T

7. $\sim p \rightarrow q$

p	q	$\sim p$	$\sim p \rightarrow q$
T	T	F	T
T	F	F	T
F	T	T	T
F	F	T	F

9. $\sim \sim p \vee q$

p	q	$\sim \sim p$	$\sim \sim p \vee q$
T	T	T	T
T	F	T	T
F	T	F	T
F	F	F	F

10. $\sim \sim p \rightarrow \sim \sim q$

p	q	$\sim \sim p$	$\sim \sim q$	$\sim \sim p \rightarrow \sim \sim q$
T	T	T	T	T
T	F	T	F	F
F	T	F	T	T
F	F	F	F	T

Exercise 6-8

1. Valid

a & b
∴ *a*

a	b	a & b	a
T	T	T	T
T	F	F	T
F	T	F	F
F	F	F	F

3. Invalid
p v *q*
p
∴ ~ *q*

p	q	p v q	p	~ q
T	T	T	T	F
T	F	T	T	T
F	T	T	F	F
F	F	F	F	T

4. Invalid
p → q
~ *p*
∴ *q*

p	q	p → q	~ p	q
T	T	T	F	T
T	F	F	F	F
F	T	T	T	T
F	F	T	T	F

58

5. Valid

a & b
$\sim a$
$\therefore b$

a	b	a & b	~ a	b
T	T	T	F	T
T	F	F	F	F
F	T	F	T	T
F	F	F	T	F

6. Invalid

$p \rightarrow q$
$q \rightarrow r$
$\therefore q$

p	q	r	p → q	q → r	q
T	T	T	T	T	T
T	T	F	T	F	T
T	F	T	F	T	F
T	F	F	F	T	F
F	T	T	T	T	T
F	T	F	T	F	T
F	F	T	T	T	F
F	F	F	T	T	F

8. Valid

$a \lor (b$ & $c)$
$\sim (b$ & $c)$
$\therefore a$

a	b	c	(b & c)	a v (b & c)	~ (b & c)	a
T	T	T	T	T	F	T
T	T	F	F	T	T	T
T	F	T	F	T	T	T
T	F	F	F	T	T	T
F	T	T	T	T	F	F
F	T	F	F	F	T	F
F	F	T	F	F	T	F
F	F	F	F	F	T	F

9. Valid

$x \to y$
$y \to z$
$\therefore x \to z$

x	y	z	$x \to y$	$y \to z$	$x \to z$
T	T	T	T	T	T
T	T	F	T	F	F
T	F	T	F	T	T
T	F	F	F	T	F
F	T	T	T	T	T
F	T	F	T	F	T
F	F	T	T	T	T
F	F	F	T	T	T

10. Invalid

$p \to q$
$\therefore p \to (p \,\&\, q)$

p	q	p & q	$p \to q$	$p \to (p \,\&\, q)$
T	T	T	T	T
T	F	F	F	F
F	T	F	T	T
F	F	F	T	T

11. Invalid

$a \to b$
$b \to c$
$\therefore (b \,\&\, c) \lor (a \,\&\, b)$

a	b	c	(b & c)	(a & b)	$a \to b$	$b \to c$	(b & c) v (a & b)
T	T	T	T	T	T	T	T
T	T	F	F	T	T	F	T
T	F	T	F	F	F	T	F
T	F	F	F	F	F	T	F
F	T	T	T	F	T	T	T
F	T	F	F	F	T	F	F
F	F	T	F	F	T	T	F
F	F	F	F	F	T	T	F

60

12. Invalid

$a \vee (b \to c)$
$b \,\&\, \sim c$
$\therefore \sim a$

a	b	c	$(b \to c)$	$a \vee (b \to c)$	$b \,\&\, \sim c$	$\sim a$
T	T	T	T	T	F	F
T	T	F	F	T	T	F
T	F	T	T	T	F	F
T	F	F	T	T	F	F
F	T	T	T	T	F	T
F	T	F	F	F	T	T
F	F	T	T	T	F	T
F	F	F	T	T	F	T

13. Valid

$(p \vee q) \to (p \,\&\, q)$
$p \,\&\, q$
$\therefore p \vee q$

p	q	$(p \vee q)$	$(p \,\&\, q)$	$(p \vee q) \to (p \,\&\, q)$	$p \,\&\, q$	$p \vee q$
T	T	T	T	T	T	T
T	F	T	F	F	F	T
F	T	T	F	F	F	T
F	F	F	F	T	F	F

15. Valid

$(d \vee e) \to (d \,\&\, e)$
$\sim (d \vee e)$
$\therefore \sim (d \,\&\, e)$

d	e	$(d \vee e)$	$(d \,\&\, e)$	$(d \vee e) \to (d \,\&\, e)$	$\sim (d \vee e)$	$\sim (d \,\&\, e)$
T	T	T	T	T	F	F
T	F	T	F	F	F	T
F	T	T	F	F	F	T
F	F	F	F	T	T	T

16. Valid

$(p \to q) \to (p \to r)$
$\sim (p \to q)$
$\sim r$
$\therefore p$

p	q	r	$(p \to q)$	$(p \to r)$	$(p \to q) \to (p \to r)$	$\sim (p \to q)$	$\sim r$	p
T	T	T	T	T	T	F	F	T
T	T	F	T	F	F	F	T	T
T	F	T	F	T	T	T	F	T
T	F	F	F	F	T	T	T	T
F	T	T	T	T	T	F	F	F
F	T	F	T	T	T	F	T	F
F	F	T	T	T	T	F	F	F
F	F	F	T	T	T	F	T	F

17. Valid

$(d \vee e) \to f$
$f \to (d \,\&\, e)$
$\therefore (d \,\&\, e) \to (d \vee e)$

d	e	f	$(d \vee e)$	$(d \,\&\, e)$	$(d \vee e) \to f$	$f \to (d \,\&\, e)$	$(d \,\&\, e) \to (d \vee e)$
T	T	T	T	T	T	T	T
T	T	F	T	T	F	T	T
T	F	T	T	F	T	F	T
T	F	F	T	F	F	T	T
F	T	T	T	F	T	F	T
F	T	F	T	F	F	T	T
F	F	T	F	F	T	F	T
F	F	F	F	F	T	T	T

18. Invalid

$\sim (d \,\&\, e)$
$e \vee f$
$\therefore \sim d \,\&\, e$

d	e	f	$(d \,\&\, e)$	$e \vee f$	$\sim (d \,\&\, e)$	$e \vee f$	$\sim d \,\&\, e$
T	T	T	T	T	F	T	F
T	T	F	T	T	F	T	F
T	F	T	F	T	T	T	F
T	F	F	F	F	T	F	F
F	T	T	F	T	T	T	T
F	T	F	F	T	T	T	T
F	F	T	F	T	T	T	F
F	F	F	F	F	T	F	F

19. Invalid

$d \mathbin{\&} (\sim e \to \sim d)$
$f \to \sim e$
$\therefore f$

d	e	f	(~e→~d)	f→~e	d & (~e→~d)	f→~e	f
T	T	T	T	F	T	F	T
T	T	F	T	T	T	T	F
T	F	T	F	T	F	T	T
T	F	F	F	T	F	T	F
F	T	T	T	F	F	F	T
F	T	F	T	T	F	T	F
F	F	T	T	T	F	T	T
F	F	F	T	T	F	T	F

20. Invalid

$d \lor \sim e$
$f \to e$
$\therefore d \to \sim f$

d	e	f	d v ~e	f→e	d→~f
T	T	T	T	T	F
T	T	F	T	T	T
T	F	T	T	F	F
T	F	F	T	T	T
F	T	T	F	T	T
F	T	F	F	T	T
F	F	T	T	F	T
F	F	F	T	T	T

Exercise 6-9

1. Valid

$\sim p \to q$

$q \to \sim r$

$\sim q$

$\therefore p$

p	q	r	$\sim p \to q$	$q \to \sim r$	$\sim q$	p
T	T	T	T	F	F	T
T	T	F	T	T	F	T
T	F	T	T	T	T	T
T	F	F	T	T	T	T
F	T	T	T	F	F	F
F	T	F	T	T	F	F
F	F	T	F	T	T	F
F	F	F	F	T	T	F

2. Valid

$p \to q$

$\sim p \to r$

$\sim p$

$\therefore r$

p	q	r	$p \to q$	$\sim p \to r$	$\sim p$	r
T	T	T	T	T	F	T
T	T	F	T	T	F	F
T	F	T	F	T	F	T
T	F	F	F	T	F	F
F	T	T	T	T	T	T
F	T	F	T	F	T	F
F	F	T	T	T	T	T
F	F	F	T	F	T	F

4. Valid

$c \vee f$

$\sim f$

$\therefore c$

c	f	$c \vee f$	$\sim f$	c
T	T	T	F	T
T	F	T	T	T
F	T	T	F	F
F	F	F	T	F

5. Invalid

$f \rightarrow s$
$s \rightarrow p$
$\therefore p$

f	s	p		$f \rightarrow s$	$s \rightarrow p$	p
T	T	T		T	T	T
T	T	F		T	F	F
T	F	T		F	T	T
T	F	F		F	T	F
F	T	T		T	T	T
F	T	F		T	F	F
F	F	T		T	T	T
F	F	F		T	T	F

6. Invalid

$w \vee t$
$j \vee \sim j$
$w \rightarrow j$
$\therefore \sim j$

w	t	j		$w \vee t$	$j \vee \sim j$	$w \rightarrow j$	$\sim j$
T	T	T		T	T	T	F
T	T	F		T	T	F	T
T	F	T		T	T	T	F
T	F	F		T	T	F	T
F	T	T		T	T	F	F
F	T	F		T	T	F	T
F	F	T		F	T	F	F
F	F	F		F	T	F	T

7. Invalid

$m \rightarrow \sim p$
$\sim p \rightarrow m$
$\therefore \sim p \ \& \ m$

m	p	$m \rightarrow \sim p$	$\sim p \rightarrow m$	$\sim p \ \& \ m$
T	T	F	T	F
T	F	T	T	T
F	T	T	T	F
F	F	T	F	F

8. Valid

c v e
~ c
∴ *e*

c	e	c v e	~ c	e
T	T	T	F	T
T	F	T	F	F
F	T	T	T	T
F	F	F	T	F

9. Valid

w v ~ w
~ w → ~ r
w → r
~ w
∴ *~ r*

w	r	w v ~ w	~ w → ~ r	w → r	~ w	~ r
T	T	T	T	T	F	F
T	F	T	T	F	F	T
F	T	T	F	T	T	F
F	F	T	T	T	T	T

10. Invalid

h v p
p → w
h
∴ *~ w*

h	p	w	h v p	p → w	h	~ w
T	T	T	T	T	T	F
T	T	F	T	F	T	T
T	F	T	T	T	T	F
T	F	F	T	T	T	T
F	T	T	T	T	F	F
F	T	F	T	F	F	T
F	F	T	T	T	F	F
F	F	F	F	T	F	T

Exercise 6-10

1. Valid
a & b
∴ *a*

F		F	
a & b		**a**	
F F		F	

5. Valid
a & b
~ *a*
∴ *b*

F	T	F
a & b	**~ a**	**b**
F F	F	F

9. Valid
x → y
y → z
∴ *x → z*

F	T	F
x → y	**y → z**	**x → z**
T F	F F	T F

16. Valid
(*p → q*) → (*p → r*)
~ (*p → q*)
~ *r*
∴ *p*

T	F	T	F
(p → q) → (p →r)	**~ (p → q)**	**~r**	**p**
F F F	F	F	F

18. Invalid
~ (*d & e*)
e v *f*
∴ ~ *d & e*

T	T	F
~ (d & e)	**e v f**	**~ d & e**
F	F T	F

TEST BANK

Multiple Choice
(Correct answers are marked with an asterisk.)

1. Propositional logic is the branch of deductive reasoning that deals with the logical relationships among…
    a. Predicates
    b. Arguments
    c. Disjunctions
    * d. Statements

2. The four logical connectives are…
    a. Conjuctions, conditionals, compounds, and disjunctions
    b. Conjunctions, statements, disjuncts, conditionals
    *c. Conditionals, disjunctions, negations, and conjuctions
    d. Conjuncts, disjuncts, conditionals, and negations

3. The symbolization for a conditional is…
    a. $p \vee q$
    * b. $p \rightarrow q$
    c. $p * q$
    d. $p \ \& \ q$

4. A conditional is false only when the antecedent is…
    * a. True and the consequent is false
    b. False and the consequent is false
    c. True and the consequent is true
    d. False and the consequent is true

5. In a conditional statement, "only if" introduces…
    a. A conjunct
    b. The antecedent
    * c. The consequent
    d. A disjunct

6. In a conditional statement, "unless" means "if not" and introduces…
    a. A negation
    b. The conjunct
    c. The consequent
    * d. The antecedent

7. The truth-table test of validity is based on the fact that it's impossible for a valid argument to have true premises and ...
    a. A true conclusion
    b. A negated conclusion
    c. A conditional
    * d. A false conclusion

8. The truth value of a compound statement depends on the truth values of...
    * a. Its components
    b. The rest of the argument
    c. Its disjuncts
    d. The conclusion

9. "It is not the case that the car is red and the truck is blue" can be symbolized by...
    a. $\sim p \;\&\; q$
    b. $\sim (p \lor q)$
    * c. $\sim (p \;\&\; q)$
    d. $\sim p \;\&\; \sim q$

10. The argument known as affirming the consequent is symbolized by...
    * a.
$$p \rightarrow q$$
$$q$$
$$\therefore p$$

    b.
$$p \rightarrow q$$
$$p$$
$$\therefore q$$

    c.
$$p \rightarrow q$$
$$\sim p$$
$$\therefore \sim q$$

    d.
$$p \rightarrow q$$
$$\sim q$$
$$\therefore \sim p$$

True/False
(Correct answers marked with an asterisk.)

1. Propositional logic uses symbols to stand not just for statements but also for the relationships between statements.
        * a. True
        b. False

2. The symbol used to indicate a negation is &.
        a. True
        * b. False

3. Each of the component statements in a conjunction is called a disjunct.
        a. True
        *b. False

4. If just one statement in a conjunction is false, the whole conjunction is still true.
        a. True
        * b. False

5. If only one statement in a disjunction is true, the whole disjunction is false.
        a. True
        * b. False

6. A double negation is the same thing as no negation.
        * a. True
        b. False

7. The truth table for a two-variable argument has eight rows.
        a. True
        * b. False

8. The first step in the short method is to write out the symbolized argument in a single row.
        * a. True
        b. False

9. The following is an accurate truth table for a conjunction:

p	q	p & q
T	T	T
T	F	F
F	T	F
F	F	F

     *a. True
     b. False

10. The following is an accurate truth table for a conditional:

p	q	p → q
T	T	T
T	F	F
F	T	T
F	F	T

     * a. True
     b. False

Short Answer/Short Essay

1. What are the four connectives in propositional logic, how are they symbolized, and what do they mean?

2. How do parentheses change the meaning of symbolized statements?

3. What is the rationale behind the short method of argument evaluation?

4. What are the four steps of the short method?

5. Under what conditions is a conditional statement true?

6. What is a truth table and how does it help you determine the validity of arguments?

7. If an argument form is valid, what does that imply about other arguments using the same form? How does that fact help you evaluate arguments?

8. What is the difference between the inclusive and the exclusive interpretations of a disjunction?

9. In propositional logic, what English words are equivalent to the symbol &?

10. What is the difference between simple and compound statements?

Chapter 7
Deductive Reasoning: Categorical Logic

Like the last chapter (propositional logic), this one requires a lot of close attention from students as well as a good deal of practice. The chapter's exercises are best viewed as starting points on the learning curve. They can be supplemented with (1) in-class exercises in which students get a chance to check and challenge each other's work, (2) class demonstrations in which the instructor works through claim translations and argument evaluations, and (3) whatever opportunities for practice are available (including those to be found in the online Study Guide).

CHAPTER SUMMARY

Every categorical statement has a subject term and a predicate term. There are four standard forms of categorical statements: (1) universal affirmative ("All dogs are mammals"); (2) universal negative ("No dogs are mammals"); (3) particular affirmative ("Some dogs are mammals"); and (4) particular negative (Some dogs are not mammals").

Categorical statements must be translated into standard form before you can work with them. Translating involves identifying terms and ensuring that they designate classes and determining the quantifiers. Drawing Venn diagrams is a good way to visualize categorical statements and to tell whether one statement is equivalent to another.

A categorical syllogism is an argument consisting of three categorical statements (two premises and a conclusion) that are interlinked in s structured way. The syllogism consists of a major term, minor term, and middle term. The middle term appears once in each premise. The major term appears in one premise and the conclusion, and the minor term appears in the other premise and the conclusion. You can use Venn diagrams to represent categorical statements, showing how the terms are related.

The easiest way to check the validity of a categorical syllogism is to draw a three-circle Venn diagram—three overlapping circles with the relationship between terms graphically indicated. If, after diagramming each premise, the diagram reflects what's asserted in the conclusion, the argument is valid. If not, the argument is invalid.

EXERCISES NOT ANSWERED IN THE TEXT

Exercise 7-1

2. s=plants; p=Baptists; particular affirmative; I
3. s= cats that have lived over fifteen years in a domestic setting; p= pets free of all health problems; universal negative; E
4. s=mammals; p=whales; particular negative; O
6. s=football players; p=A-students; universal negative; E
7. s= refugees from unstable countries; p=poor people; universal affirmative; A
9. s= taxpayers from the 2003 tax year; p=embezzlers; universal negative; E
10. s= U.S. prosecutors who have reviewed the cases of death and injury at the Ace-Westinghouse foundry; p= friends of corporate America; universal negative; E

11. s= All cancer survivors in the clinical study; p= coffee drinkers; universal affirmative; A
13. s= pro-democracy students in China; p=outside agitators; universal negative; E
14. s= congressional Republican leaders; p=pro-lifers; particular affirmative; I
15. s= health care programs proposed in the Senate; p=viable options; particular negative; O
17. s= child-abuse caseworkers; p=overburdened civil servants; universal affirmative; A

Exercise 7-2

2. Some government programs are things that are wasteful. I
3. All soldiers who give their all are persons who are brave. A
4. All whispering people are liars. A
6. All rock and roll songs are things that have a back beat. A
7. Some people with pinched faces are persons who have poisonous hearts. I
8. No snakes are mammals. E
10. All good humans are dead humans. A
11. All persons identical with Gregory are Republicans. A
12. No soldiers who broke their legs are soldiers who finished their training. E
14. All excellent things are things with difficulty. A
15. All persons identical with Jonathan are persons who are not very brave pilots. A
16. All men are persons who have sinned. A

Exercise 7-3

2. All earthquakes are potential disasters. A
3. All persons who wish to salute the free and independent side of their evolutionary character are persons who acquire cats. A
6. Some young people are non-Catholics. O
7. All political parties that get at least 50 percent of the vote in a presidential election are major players in American politics. A
9. Some products advertised on the internet are unsafe devices. I
10. All persons who love only once in their lives are…shallow people. A
11. Some of the members of the Daughters of the American Revolution are persons from Canada. I
13. Some socialists are not communists. O
14. All prejudices are things that may be traced to the intestines. A
16. All persons who seek the truth through philosophy are free persons. A
17. No persons born to be hanged are persons who shall be drowned. E
18. All visionaries are artists. A
19. Some writers are not poets. O

Exercise 7-4

2. No creed can be inviolable. = No creeds are inviolable things. s=creeds; p= inviolable things.

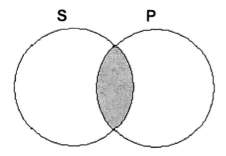

3. No one can join the army when they're sixteen. = No persons are people who can join the army when they're sixteen. s=persons; p= people who can join the army when they're sixteen.

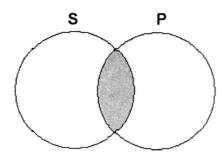

4. Some birds are flightless. = Some birds are flightless birds. s=birds; p= flightless birds.

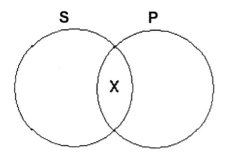

6. Abraham Lincoln is one of the few writers whose words helped turn the world. = All persons identical with Abraham Lincoln are writers whose words helped turn the world. s = All persons identical with Abraham Lincoln; p = writers whose words helped turn the world.

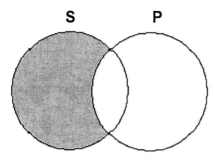

7. Some snakes are not poisonous. = Some snakes are not poisonous snakes. s= snakes; p = poisonous snakes.

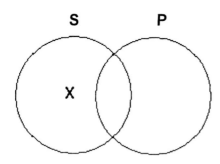

9. It is false that some businessmen are crooks. = No businessmen are crooks. s= businessmen; p = crooks.

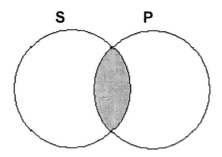

10. Some people with excellent reputations are not persons of excellent character.= Some people with excellent reputations are not persons of excellent character. s = people with excellent reputations; p = not persons of excellent character.

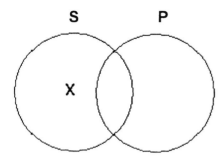

11. Black dogs didn't get fed. = No black dogs are dogs that got fed. s = black dogs; p = dogs that got fed.

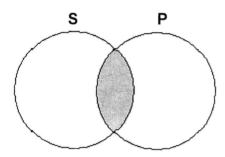

13. Rainbows are always misleading. = All rainbows are misleading things. s = rainbows; p = misleading things.

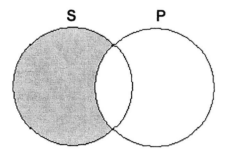

14. There are bad apples in every barrel. = Some bad apples are apples in every barrel. s = bad apples; p = apples in every barrel.

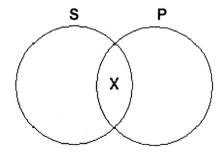

15. Few friendships could survive the moodiness of love affairs. = Some friendships are not friendships that could survive the moodiness of love affairs. s = friendships; p = friendships that could not survive the moodiness of love affairs.

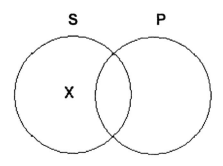

Exercise 7-5

2. Equivalent

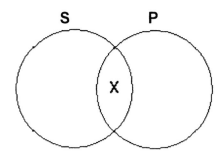 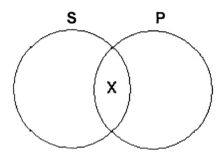

4. Equivalent

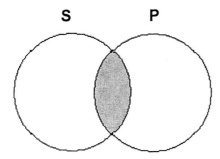

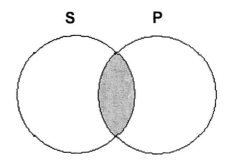

5. Not Equivalent

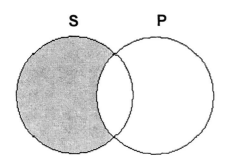

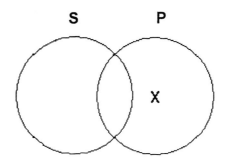

7. Equivalent

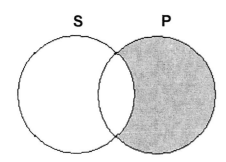

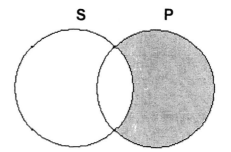

8. Equivalent

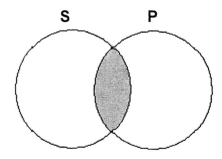 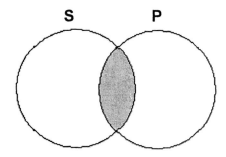

10. Equivalent

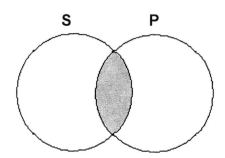 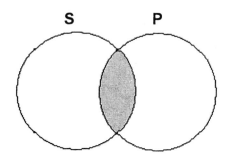

Exercise 7-6

1. No apples are vegetables. Some plants are vegetables. So some plants are not apples.
P=apples; S=plants; M=vegetables.
No P are M.
Some S are M.
Therefore, some S are not P.

3. All cars are self-propelled vehicles, and all motorcycles are self-propelled vehicles. Thus, all motorcycles are cars. P=cars; S=motorcycles; M= self-propelled vehicles.
All P are M.
All S are M.
Therefore, all S are P.

4. Some roses are yellow flowers. All roses are plants. Therefore, some plants are yellow flowers. P=yellow flowers; S=plants; M=roses.
Some M are P.
All M are S.
Therefore, some S are P.

5. All roads are highways to Rome, but no mere paths are roads. So no mere paths are highways to Rome. P=highways to Rome; S=mere paths; M=roads.
All M are P.
No S are M.
Therefore, no S are P.

7. All presidents are leaders, but some statesmen are not presidents. So some statesmen are not leaders. P=leaders; S=statesmen; M=presidents.
All M are P
Some S are not M.
Therefore, some S are not P.

8. All politicians are campaigners. All campaigners are money-grubbers. Therefore all politicians are money-grubbers. P=money grubbers; S=politicians; M=campaigners.
All S are M.
All M are P.
Therefore, all S are P.

10. All thieves are criminals. All thieves are dangers to society. Therefore, all dangers to society are criminals. P=criminals; S=dangers to society; M=thieves.
All M are P.
All M are S.
Therefore, all S are P.

Exercise 7-7

1. Valid

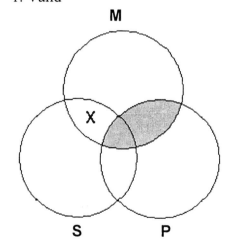

3. Invalid

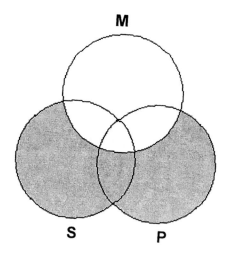

4. Valid

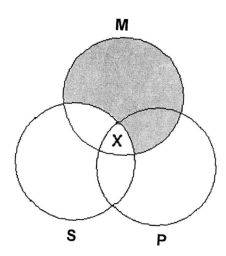

5. Invalid

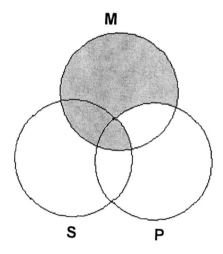

7. Invalid

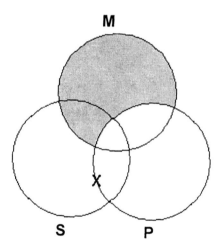

8. Valid

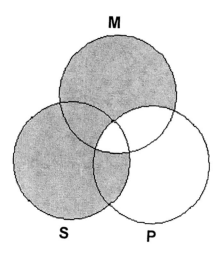

10. Invalid

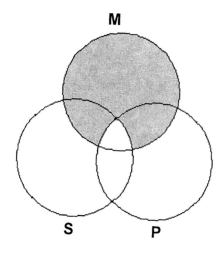

Exercise 7-8

2.
Some (P) heart-attack-inducing foods are not (M) high-fat foods.
All (S) bacon burgers are (M) high-fat foods.
Therefore, all (S) bacon burgers are (P) heart-attack-inducing foods.

Some P are M.
All S are M.
Therefore, all S are P.

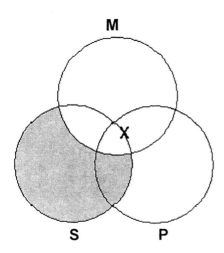

Invalid

4.

Some (S) famous men are not (P) racists since all (P) racists are (M) enemies of justice, and some (S) famous men are not (M) enemies of justice.

All P are M.
Some S are not M.
Therefore, some S are not P.

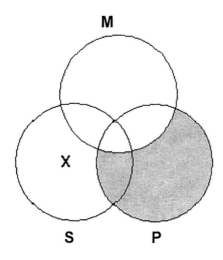

Valid

5. No (S) persons who are true to the values of this republic are (P) politicians because all (P) politicians are (M) self-promoting egoists. And no (M) self-promoting egoists are (S) persons true to the values of this republic.

All P are M.
No M are S.
Therefore, no S are P.

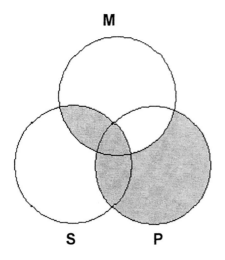

Valid

6. Some (P) philosophers are (M) musicians. Therefore, some (S) trumpet players are (P) philosophers since all (S) trumpet players are (M) musicians.

All S are M.
Some P are M.
Therefore, some S are P.

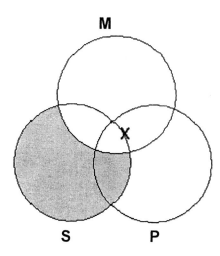

Invalid

7. All (S) opponents of the United States going to war against terrorist states are (M) people opposed to anti-terrorist security arrangements. Some (M) people opposed to anti-terrorist security arrangements are (P) Leftist extremists. Therefore, some (S) opponents of the United States going to war against terrorist states are not (P) Leftist extremists.

All S are M.
Some M are P.
Therefore, some S are not P.

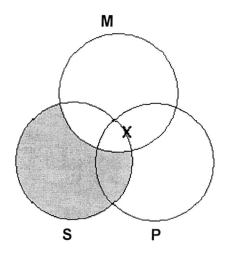

Invalid

9. Most (S) people who drive SUVs (sport utility vehicles) are (M) instant-gratification freaks who don't care about the environment or environmental issues. (M) Instant-gratification freaks who don't care about the environment or environmental issues are (P) the true enemies of the planet. Therefore, (S) people who drive SUVs are (P) the true enemies of the planet.

Some S are M.
All M are P.
Therefore, all S are P.

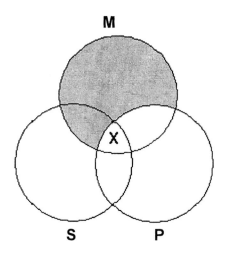

Invalid

10. (S) Vitamin pills are (M) useless gimmicks promoted as sure-cures for a variety of illnesses. Some (M) useless gimmicks promoted as sure-cures, though, are (P) placebos that can make people feel good even if they don't cure anything. So some (S) vitamin pills are (P) placebos that can make people feel good even if they don't cure anything.

All S are M.
Some M are P.
Therefore, some S are P.

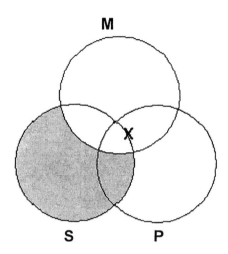

Invalid

TEST BANK

Multiple Choice
(Correct answers are marked with an asterisk.)

1. The basic unit of concern in categorical logic is the...
    a. Statement
    b. Predicate
    * c. Statement component
    d. Subject

2. The four standard forms of categorical statements are...
    a. All S are P; Some S are P; Some S are not P; All S are S
    b. All S are P; Some S are P; All S are not P; Some S are not P
    c. All S are P; No S are not P; No S are P; All P are S
    * d. All S are P; Some S are P; Some S are not P; No S are P

3. The standard form statement No S are P is a...
    *a. Universal negative
    b. Universal affirmative
    c. Particular affirmative
    d. Particular negative

4. A particular negative statement is designated by the letter...
    a. I
    * b. O
    c. A
    d. E

5. The pattern of standard-form categorical statements is...
    a. Subject term, copula, predicate term, quantifier
    b. Subject term, copula, negative term, quantifier
    * c. Quantifier, subject term, copula, predicate term
    d. Quantifier, subject term, predicate term, copula

6. In an A-statement, the words "only" and "only if" precede the ...
    a. Subject term
    b. Negative term
    c. Quantifier term
    *d. Predicate term

7. The singular statement "John Brown is a plumber" is translated into the following A-statement...
    a. All persons like John Brown are plumbers.
    b. No persons like John Brown are Plumbers
    c. John Brown is a person identical with a plumber.
    * d. All persons identical with John Brown are plumbers.

8. A syllogism is a deductive argument made up of...
    * a. Three statements—two premises and a conclusion
    b. Three statements—three premises and a conclusion
    c. Two universal statements and one particular statement
    d. A conclusion and two affirmative premises

9. A categorical syllogism has...
    a. Exactly three terms, with each one appearing three times in the argument.
    * b. Exactly three terms, with each one appearing twice in the argument.
    c. Exactly three terms, with each one appearing once in the argument
    d. Exactly two terms, with each one appearing three times in the argument.

10. The easiest way to check the validity of a categorical syllogism is to …
    a. Draw a four-circle Venn diagram.
    b. Create a truth table
    * c. Draw a three-circle Venn diagram.
    d. Draw a two-circle Venn diagram.

True/False
(Correct answers marked with an asterisk.)

1. In a categorical syllogism, the middle term appears in each premise but not the conclusion.
    * a. True
    b. False

2. In a categorical syllogism, the major term appears as the predicate term in the conclusion and also in one of the premises.
    *a. True
    b. False

3. "Some S are not P" is an I-statement.
    a. True
    *b. False

4. "No S are P" is an O-statement.
    a. True
    * b. False

5. "All cars are not Fords" is expressed in standard form.
    a. True
    * b. False

6. In an A-statement, the words "the only" precede the subject term.
    * a. True
    b. False

7. "All trucks are Chevrolets" is a universal negative statement.
    a. True
    * b. False

8. The copula is always either "are" or "are not."
    * a. True
    b. False

9. In categorical statements, "some" means "at least one."
    *a. True
    b. False

10. When checking the validity of a categorical syllogism, if the Venn diagram reflects the assertion in the conclusion, the argument is valid :

    * a. True
    b. False

Short Answer/Short Essay

1. What are the four standard forms of categorical statements?

2. What is the main purpose of translating categorical statements into standard form?

3. What are the four parts of a categorical syllogism and what is the function of each one?

4. What are singular statements and how are they dealt with when translating them into standard form?

5. In logic, what is the meaning of "some" and what is the advantage of using this restrictive definition?

6. How can you use Venn diagrams to determine whether two categorical statements are equivalent?

7. What are the basic steps in using Venn diagrams to check the validity of categorical syllogisms?

8. What is the proper place for minor, major, and middle terms in a categorical syllogism?

9. When diagramming a categorical syllogism with a universal premise and a particular premise, why is it important to diagram the universal premise first?

10. What are the two qualities that can be expressed in categorical statements and to what do they refer?

Chapter 8
Inductive Reasoning

This chapter is one of the more versatile in the text. It can be used at almost any point in the course after Chapter 1 (or better, Chapter 3). Students are not likely to find this chapter difficult whether it appears very early in the course or very late. It makes a good prologue to Chapter 10 (Judging Scientific Theories). And it can be a very helpful part of a solid course in arguments that follows this textual thread: Chapter 1, Chapter 3, and Chapters 6 through 9.

CHAPTER SUMMARY

An inductive argument is intended to provide only probable support for its conclusion, being considered strong if it succeeds in providing such support and weak if it does not.

Inductive arguments come in several forms, including enumerative, analogical, and causal. In enumerative induction, we argue from premises about some members of a group to a generalization about the entire group. The entire group is called the target group; the observed members of the group, the sample; and the group characteristics we're interested in, the relevant property. An enumerative induction can fail to be strong by having a sample that's too small or not representative. When we draw a conclusion about a target group based on an inadequate sample size, we're said to commit the error of hasty generalization. Opinion polls are enumerative inductive arguments, or the basis of enumerative inductive arguments, and must be judged by the same general criteria used to judge any other enumerative induction.

In analogical induction, or argument by analogy, we reason that since two or more things are similar in several respects, they must be similar in some further respect. We evaluate arguments by analogy according to several criteria: (1) the number of relevant similarities between things being compared, (2) the number of relevant dissimilarities, (3) the number of instances (or cases) of similarities or dissimilarities, and (4) the diversity among the cases.

A causal argument is an inductive argument whose conclusion contains a causal claim. There are several inductive patterns of reasoning used to assess causal connections. These include the Method of Agreement, the Method of Difference, the Method of Agreement and Difference, and the Method of Concomitant Variation. Errors in cause-and-effect reasoning are common. They include misidentifying relevant factors in a causal process, overlooking relevant factors, confusing cause with coincidence, confusing cause with temporal order, and mixing up cause and effect.

Crucial to an understanding of cause-and-effect relationships are the notions of necessary and sufficient conditions. A necessary condition for the occurrence of an event is one without which the event cannot occur. A sufficient condition for the occurrence of an event is one that guarantees that the event occurs.

EXERCISES NOT ANSWERED IN THE TEXT

Exercise 8-1

2. *Target group*: people in general; *sample*: people on the street who have been questioned by TV reporters; *relevant property*: being fed up with celebrities who voice their opinions. The argument is weak. The sample is not representative and is also probably too small.

3. *Target group*: medical treatments; *sample*: two cases in which proposed treatments turned out to be ineffective; *relevant property*: treatments turning out to be worthless. The argument is weak. The sample is too small.

5. *Target group*: American adults; *sample*: several thousand gun owners; *relevant property*: being opposed to gun-control laws. The argument is weak. The sample is not representative.

6. *Target group*: future Buffalo winters; *sample*: the past 20 Buffalo winters; *relevant property*: Buffalo's receiving several feet of snow. The argument is strong.

7. *Target group*: crimes committed in Chicago; *sample*: Chicago crimes reported in newspapers; *relevant property*: crimes committed by racial minorities. The argument is weak because the sample is not likely to be representative. Newspaper reports of crimes may not reflect the actual incidence of crimes.

9. *Target group*: water in the Charles river; *sample*: two hundred samples of water taken from many sites all along the Charles river; *relevant property*: concentrations of toxic chemicals. The argument is strong.

10. *Target group*: children; *sample*: children reported by the news media to have been abducted in the past year; *relevant property*: being abducted. The argument is weak. The sample is not representative (and probably too small) since reports of the news media are not likely to reflect the true incidence of abductions.

11. *Target group*: university fraternities; *sample*: at least two fraternities involved in illegal activity; *relevant property*: illegal activity involving fraternities. The argument is weak. The sample is much too small.

Exercise 8-2

2. Weak. The argument could be strengthened by polling a truly representative sample of subjects, say, 1,200 (if the poll is to be national in scope) or far fewer if the argument concerns a smaller subgroup (perhaps people who live in a particular neighborhood).

3. Weak. The argument could be strengthened by including in the sample a much larger list of treatments (perhaps a hundred or more) drawn from the last twenty or thirty years of medical practice.

5. Weak. The argument could be strengthened by discarding the very unrepresentative sample of gun owners and instead polling a representative sample of adults (1,000-1,500), whose views on gun-control laws are likely to be more reflective of the nation as a whole.

6. Strong. The argument would be weakened considerably if the sample was limited to only one previous Buffalo winter.

7. Weak. The argument could be strengthened by discarding the newspaper reports and using police records instead. Even this improved poll may be misleading, however, because the crime rate may be more closely linked to factors such as income or social status than membership in a minority.

9. Strong. The argument would be weakened if the samples were drawn from just one site.

10. Weak. The argument could be strengthened by using national crime statistics rather than news reports—especially if the statistics are drawn from, say, the past ten years.

11. Weak. The argument could be strengthened by examining the criminal records of a large number of fraternity brothers belonging to a much broader sample of fraternities.

Exercise 8-3

2. The poll does not support Anita's conclusion. The sample is neither random nor representative. The people interviewed actually attended a musical and are therefore self-selected. And, because of their attendance, we may surmise that they are likely to be predisposed toward the arts—unlike many other Americans.

3. The survey does not support the conclusion. The sample is not representative of women aged 25 to 45, for a large portion of the sample is skewed toward well educated, academic women. The sample is also too small to draw reliable conclusions about the entire target group of 25-to-45-year-old women. Neither is the sample random since the researcher simply chose subjects from her own group of friends and colleagues.

4. The poll does not support the pollsters' conclusion. The sample is not representative of the target group. The target group is supposed to be physicians, but the sample consists of a subspecialty of physicians—obstetrician-gynecologists.

5. The survey does not adequately support the magazine's conclusion. The sample has not been randomly selected; it has instead been self-selected. The magazine's readers—including the 20,000 respondents—may not be representative of the target group.

Exercise 8-4

2. c
3. a
4. c
5. d

Exercise 8-5

2. Slightly more likely to be true. Anita's revised sample, however, is still not entirely representative of her target group (Americans).
3. Not more likely to be true. The sociologist's sample is still not representative of the target group.
4. Much more likely to be true.
5. The conclusion is not more likely to be true because the sample, though larger, is still self-selected and still not representative of the target group.

Exercise 8-6

1. Literary analogy

3. Enumerative induction

4. Literary analogy

5. Argument by analogy. *One instance compared*: the world and a machine; *relevant similarities*: adapting of means to ends; *conclusion*: nature must be designed by an intelligence. The argument is weak because nature is not only analogous to a machine. It is also analogous to a living thing.

7. Argument by analogy. *One instance compared*: a bully and a dictator; *relevant similarities*: tolerating a bully or dictator leads to further abuse; *conclusion*: the best course of action for people oppressed by a dictator is to resist and attack. The argument is weak because dictators rarely cave in simply because there is violent resistance to their rule.

9. Literary analogy

10. Argument by analogy. *Several instances compared*: Several Chevrolets bought in the past five years; *relevant similarities*: the cars being Chevrolets, George's loving all the previous cars; *conclusion*: George will probably love the Chevrolet he bought yesterday. The argument is strong.

11. Argument by analogy. *Several instances compared*: Numerous other people; *relevant similarities*: publicly observable phenomena (behavior); *conclusion*: other people must have subjective experiences. Many philosophers would probably say that this argument is strong.

Exercise 8-7

2. *Things being compared*: situations in which the United Nations might intervene; *relevant similarities*: the United Nations being presented with an opportunity to act, impending human rights catastrophe; *diversity among multiple cases*: doesn't seem to be a significant factor here because there are only two cases under consideration; *conclusion*: The UN will not intervene to stop any widespread slaughter of innocents in Nigeria. The argument seems weak because of some dissimilarities in the analogy. Presumably the Nigerian crisis is several years removed from the other two cases; the international political climate is different; and currently the UN leadership seems to have a different attitude toward intervention in pogroms.

3. *Things being compared*: development of a person and of the human race; *relevant similarities*: both involve biological processes of great complexity taking place under "appropriate conditions" and commencing with a single cell; *diversity among multiple cases*: not a significant factor; *conclusion*: Under appropriate conditions, a cell may, in the course of untold millions of years, give origin to the human race. The argument is strong.

4. *Things being compared*: the establishment of casinos; *relevant similarities*: being a casino in and around New York State; *diversity among multiple cases*: a significant factor because existing casinos were established in very different locations and economic conditions; *conclusion*: A new casino in Buffalo will bring a tremendous amount of revenue into both area businesses and local government, without inviting the evils of organized crime and causing the degradation of law and order or quality of life. The argument seems strong (though the premises are questionable).

6. *Things being compared*: An animal and the world; *relevant similarities*: both in an animal and the world "a continual circulation of matter in it produces no disorder: a continual waste in every part is incessantly repaired: The closest sympathy is perceived throughout the whole system. And each part or member, in performing its proper offices, operates both to its own preservation and to that of the whole"; *diversity among multiple cases*: not a significant factor; *conclusion*: "The world…is an animal, and the Deity is the soul of the world, activating it and activated by it"; The argument is weak (but ingenious).

7. *Things being compared*: Inanimate objects and men who serve the state; *relevant similarities*: no exercise of judgment or moral sense, being used as physical instruments or objects; *diversity among multiple cases*: not a significant factor; *conclusion*: Such men of the state "command no more respect than men of straw, or a lump of dirt"; The argument is weak.

Exercise 8-8

1. *Conclusion*: Something about staying in that ward is the cause of the prolonged illness. Method of agreement. Strong.

3. *Conclusion*: An experimental vaccine prevented women from becoming persistently infected with a [type of human papilloma virus called HPV-16] that is associated with half of all cervical cancers. Joint method of agreement and difference. Strong.

4. *Conclusion*: Getting the endorsement of the teachers union in this town is absolutely essential to being elected to the school board in this city. Method of difference. Strong.

5. *Conclusion*: The number of weekly disciplinary actions decreased because the Ten Commandments were posted in the hallway outside the principal's office. Method of agreement. Weak. (Many other factors could have affected the number of disciplinary actions besides recent changes in the school. Other possible factors are parental involvement, normal fluctuations in the rate of misbehavior, the beginning of a sports season, etc.)

6. *Conclusion*: Y caused E. Joint method of agreement and difference. Strong.

8. *Conclusion*: Oranges and lemons were the most effective remedies for the illness. Joint method of agreement and difference. Strong.

9. *Conclusion*: Johnny's brother was the cause of this outbreak. Method of difference. Strong.

10. *Conclusion*: The extra calcium caused the increased density. Joint method of agreement and difference. Strong.

11. *Conclusion*: The new traffic light has made quite a difference. Method of difference. Strong.

12. *Conclusion*: There's a causal connection between serum cholesterol levels and risk of atherosclerosis. Correlation. Strong.

14. *Conclusion*: The reason there has been so many terrorist attacks in Western countries in the past ten years is that the rights of Palestinians have been violated by Westerners. Method of agreement. Strong.

15. *Conclusion*: Charlie is upset because he got word that his grades weren't good enough to get into med school. Method of difference. Weak.

17. *Conclusion*: Running a major appliance interferes with my TV reception. Method of difference. Strong.

18. *Conclusion*: Lather-Up is better at killing germs. Joint method of agreement and difference. Strong.

20. *Conclusion*: Jackie M's criminal behavior is caused by high outdoor temperatures. Correlation. Weak.

Exercise 8-9

1. Misidentifying or overlooking relevant factors.

3. Misidentifying or overlooking relevant factors.

4. Misidentifying or overlooking relevant factors; being misled by coincidence; falling for the *post hoc* fallacy.

5. Misidentifying or overlooking relevant factors; being misled by coincidence; falling for the *post hoc* fallacy.

6. Being misled by coincidence.

8. Being misled by coincidence; falling for the *post hoc* fallacy.

9. Misidentifying or overlooking relevant factors; falling for the *post hoc* fallacy.

10. Misidentifying or overlooking relevant factors.

11. Falling for the *post hoc* fallacy; misidentifying or overlooking relevant factors.

12. Confusing cause and effect.

14. Misidentifying or overlooking relevant factors; being misled by coincidence; falling for the *post hoc* fallacy; confusing cause and effect.

15. Misidentifying or overlooking relevant factors; being misled by coincidence; falling for the *post hoc* fallacy.

17. Misidentifying or overlooking relevant factors; being misled by coincidence.

18. Misidentifying or overlooking relevant factors; falling for the *post hoc* fallacy.

20. Misidentifying or overlooking relevant factors; being misled by coincidence.

Exercise 8-10

2. d
3. a
5. b
6. b
7. c
8. d
10. d

TEST BANK

Multiple Choice
(Correct answers are marked with an asterisk.)

1. When we begin with observations about some members of a group and then generalize about all of them, we use a kind of reasoning known as...
    a. Analogical induction
    b. Causal induction
    * c. Enumerative induction
    d. Enumerative deduction

2. In enumerative induction, the whole collection of individuals being examined is called the...
    a. Sample
    * b. Target group
    c. Relevant property
    d. Control group

3. An enumerative inductive argument can fail to be strong because...
    *a. The sample is too small or not representative
    b. The target group is large
    c. The sample has many members
    d. The sample is representative of the target group

4. When we draw a conclusion about a target group based on an inadequate sample size, we make an error known as...
    a. Inductive fault
    b. Biased sample
    * c. Hasty generalization
    d. Representative sample

5. A sample that does not properly represent the target group is called a...
    a. Misdirected sample
    *b. Biased sample
    c. Representative sample
    d. Relevant sample

6. A sample that is selected randomly from a target group in such a way as to ensure that the sample is representative is known as a...
    a. Targeted sample
    b. Negative sample
    c. Empty sample
    * d. Random sample

7. A self-selecting sample is...
    a. Guaranteed to be representative
    b. A good indicator of sample quality
    c. Not likely to be biased
    * d. Not likely to be representative

8. The probability that the sample will accurately represent the target group within the margin of error is called the...
    a. Margin of error
    * b. Confidence level
    c. Polling bias
    d. Random sample

9. In an argument by analogy, the more relevant similarities there are between the things being compared, the more probable the...
    * a. Conclusion
    b. Sample
    c. Margin of error
    d. Dissimilarities

10. An inductive argument whose conclusion contains a causal claim is known as...
    a. An analogical induction
    b. A necessary condition
    * c. A causal argument
    d. A sufficient argument

True/False
(Correct answers marked with an asterisk.)

1. A sufficient condition for the occurrence of an event is one that guarantees that the event occurs.
    * a. True
    b. False

2. A modified version of Mill's Method of Agreement says that if two or more occurrences of a phenomenon have only one relevant factor in common, that factor must be the cause.
    *a. True
    b. False

3. A necessary condition for the occurrence of an event is one without which the event can still occur.
    a. True
    *b. False

4. Mill's Method of Concomitant Variation says that when two events are correlated, they are rarely causally related.
    a. True
    * b. False

5. An enumerative induction has this pattern: Thing A has properties P_1, P_2, P_3 plus the property P_4. Thing B has properties P_1, P_2, and P_3. Therefore, thing B probably has property P_4.
    a. True
    * b. False

6. People are especially prone to "it can't be just coincidence" thinking because they misjudge the probabilities involved.
    * a. True
    b. False

7. In cases in which a complete set of necessary conditions constitutes a sufficient condition for an event, we say that the conditions are individually necessary and jointly sufficient for an event to occur.
    * a. True
    b. False

8. A strong enumerative induction cannot have false premises.
    a. True
    *b. False

9. People are often guilty of biased sampling through a phenomenon called selective attention.
    * a. True
    b. False

10. People are very good at selecting things in random fashion.
    a. True
    *b. False

Short Answer/Short Essay

1. What is enumerative induction and what is its argument pattern?

2. What is the difference between target group, sample members, and relevant property?

3. In what two major ways can an enumerative inductive argument fail to be strong?

4. What is the error known as hasty generalization (give a definition and an example)?

5. What is random sampling? What does it mean to randomly select a sample from the target group?

6. What is the difference between a literary analogy and an argument by analogy? What is the purpose of each?

7. What is the difference between an enumerative induction and an argument by analogy?

8. What are the criteria for judging the strength of arguments by analogy and how are they applied?

9. What is a causal argument and what are Mill's criteria for judging its strength?

10. What is the *post hoc* fallacy (give a definition and an example)?

Chapter 9
Inference to the Best Explanation

Like most of the previous chapters, this one is modular. It can stand alone as a first introduction to inference to the best explanation, requiring no further ado about explanations or theories. It can also round out a course emphasizing arguments (in a pattern like this: Chapters 3, 6-9). And, as suggested by the table of contents, it can be used as the prelude to a major section on evaluation of theories (scientific and otherwise).

This material puts a heavy emphasis on using criteria to assess the worth of theories, applying a four-step procedure to make the assessment easier and more systematic, and paying close attention to some extended examples of theory evaluation. The natural complement to this approach is some well focused writing assignments or essay questions in which students are asked to run through their own theory evaluations. So the writing assignments and essay questions in this chapter should do a lot of pedagogical work. (The drawback, of course, is that the papers have to be graded.) Having students work through some theory evaluations in class (in instructor-led or group discussions, for example) may be just as useful. The two extended theory evaluations in the text ("A Doomed Flight" and "An Amazing Cure") could serve as a good starting point.

CHAPTER SUMMARY

Even though an explanation is not an argument, an explanation can be part of an argument—a powerful inductive argument known as inference to the best explanation. In inference to the best explanation, we reason from premises about a state of affairs to an explanation for that state of affairs. Such explanations are called theoretical explanations, or theories.

To be worthy of consideration, a theory must meet the minimum requirement for consistency. We use the criteria of adequacy to judge the plausibility of a theory in relation to competing theories. The best theory is the one that meets the criteria of adequacy better than any of its competitors. The criteria of adequacy are testability (whether there is some way to determine if a theory is true), fruitfulness (the number of novel predictions made), scope (the amount of diverse phenomena explained), simplicity (the number of assumptions made), and conservatism (how well a theory fits with existing knowledge).

Judging the worth of a theory is a four-step process called the TEST formula: (1) Stating the theory and checking for consistency, (2) assessing the evidence for the theory, (3) scrutinizing alternative theories, and (4) testing the theories with the criteria of adequacy.

EXERCISES NOT ANSWERED IN THE TEXT

Exercise 9-1

1. A statement or statements intended to tell why or how something is the case.

2. A form of inductive reasoning in which we reason from premises about a state of affairs to an explanation for that state of affairs.

3. Inductive

5. Inference to the best explanation:

> *Phenomenon Q.*
> *E provides the best explanation for Q.*
> *Therefore, it is probable that E is true.*

Enumerative induction:

> *X percent of the observed members of group A have property P.*
> *Therefore, X percent of all members of group A probably have property P.*

Analogical induction:

> *Thing A has properties P_1, P_2, P_3 plus the property P_4.*
> *Thing B has properties P_1, P_2, and P_3.*
> *Therefore, thing B probably has property P_4.*

6. An inference to the best explanation can be deemed strong if the explanation really is the best; it is deemed cogent if the premises are also true.

7. Teleological explanations try to explain the purpose of something, how it functions, or how it fits into a plan. Interpretive explanations concern the meaning of terms or states of affairs. Procedural explanations try to explain how something is done or how an action is carried out.

9. A theoretical explanation tries to explain why something is the way it is, why something is the case, or why something happened. A teleological explanation tries to explain the purpose or function of something. An interpretive explanation tries to explain the meaning of terms or states of affairs.

10. (Calls for a student response.)

Exercise 9-2

1. *State of affairs:* Most students dropping Professor Graham's class. *Explanation:* because he is so boring.

3. *State of affairs:* James saying that he saw a ghost in his bedroom. *Explanation:* He drinks too much and has a vivid imagination.

4. *State of affairs:* Crimes committed by high school students are increasing. *Explanation:* School districts refuse to mandate harsh punishments for criminal acts.

6. *State of affairs:* Binge drinking is on the rise at women's colleges. *Explanation:* The deans have permissive attitudes.

7. *State of affairs:* Americans are fond of the death penalty, but Europeans are not. *Explanation:* Americans just never got over the old Wild West eye-for-an-eye mentality.

9. *State of affairs:* Rock stars make more money than teachers. *Explanation:* They are smarter than teachers.

10. *State of affairs:* Global terrorism. *Explanation:* worldwide injustice and deprivation.

Exercise 9-3

1. theoretical
2. theoretical
4. non-theoretical, theoretical
5. theoretical
6. non-theoretical
8. non-theoretical, theoretical
9. non-theoretical
10. non-theoretical, theoretical
11. theoretical
13. theoretical
14. theoretical
15. non-theoretical
16. theoretical
17. theoretical, non-theoretical

Exercise 9-4

1. *Plausible*: By night, people are killing cows and removing their organs for sale to traditional medical practitioners (some of whom use dried animal organs as medicine). The thieves are careful to walk only on the tall grass so as not to leave footprints. They kill the cows by hitting them in the head with a mallet. *Not very plausible*: Space aliens are mutilating cows to practice techniques they intend to use on humans.

3. *Plausible*: During hypnosis Carl has been fantasizing about living a past life, while the hypnotist asks leading questions that implant past-life memories in Carl's mind. *Not very plausible*: Carl really has lived a past life.

4. *Plausible*: In many Islamic countries, tradition and stringent Islamic law have restricted the rights of women. *Not very plausible*: Many women in Islamic countries have fewer rights than men due to the influence of modern Western culture.

5. *Plausible*: In the 1980's, many government programs that aided poor or disabled people were cut. *Not very plausible*: In the 1980's, the number of homeless in the United States increased because many middle-class people decided they would rather live on the streets than in the suburbs.

7. *Plausible*: Teenagers are having sex at earlier ages because of a lack of effective sex education in the public schools. *Not very plausible*: Teenagers are having sex at earlier ages because parents and teachers have said that early sex is a good thing.

8. *Plausible*: A high fat intake leads to clogged arteries, which is a form of heart disease that can lead to heart attacks and other heart problems. *Not very plausible*: Bad karma.

9. *Plausible*: The number of law enforcement officers in the nation has doubled. *Not very plausible*: Something in the water is making people think twice before committing a violent crime.

Exercise 9-5

Passage 1
Phenomenon being explained: Drinking a warm glass of milk at bedtime seems to help some people fall asleep. *Suggested theory*: The tryptophan in milk increases serotonin levels, which help people fall asleep. *Plausible?*: Yes. *Alternative theory:* The act of drinking warm milk at bedtime is like counting sheep—it can relax some people, helping them fall asleep easier.

Passage 2
Phenomenon being explained: Worldwide decline in annual shark attacks. *Suggested theory*: People seem to have more of an understanding that the sea is a wild place that can be dangerous. *Plausible?*: Yes. *Alternative theory:* The number of sharks in the world's oceans has decreased.

Passage 3
Phenomenon being explained: A mysterious rise in the number of cases of non-Hodgkin lymphoma. *Suggested theory*: Long-term use of hair dye can cause this kind of cancer in women. *Plausible?*: Yes. *Alternative theory:* Increased air pollution is causing more cases of non-Hodgkin lymphoma.

Passage 4
Phenomenon being explained: The almost total incineration of a human body in an enclosed room while nearby flammable objects are unaffected by fire. *Suggested theory*: Spontaneous human combustion, the idea that under certain rare circumstances, a human body can spontaneously ignite, burn, and be almost entirely consumed. *Plausible?*: No. The spontaneous combustion of a human body has never been observed by anyone or documented by science. Given the biochemical makeup of the body, there seems to be no way that any kind of combustion could occur. *Alternative theory:* The clothes of elderly, incapacitated people catch fire (from a source of flame in the room), then the flesh slowly begins to burn, being fueled by body fat in a kind of "wick effect," eventually (after several hours) being almost entirely consumed without affecting nearby objects.

Exercise 9-6

1. No.
3. The best theory is the eligible theory that meets the criteria of adequacy better than any of its competitors.
4. The criteria of adequacy are standards used to judge the worth of explanatory theories. They include testability, fruitfulness, scope, simplicity, and conservatism.
5. A testable theory is one in which there is some way to determine whether the theory is true or false—that is, it predicts something other than what it was introduced to explain. A fruitful theory is one that makes novel predictions. A conservative theory is one that fits with our established beliefs.
7. No. Paranormal theories posit unknown entities or forces, which renders them much less simple than theories that do not posit such things.
8. The chances of the non-conservative theory being true are not good (because it has no evidence in its favor, while our well-established beliefs have plenty of evidence on their side). The conflict of beliefs (between the new theory and what we already have good reason to believe) undermines our knowledge because we cannot know something that is in doubt, and the conflict would be cause for doubt. And the conflict of beliefs lessens our understanding because the new beliefs cannot be plausibly integrated into our other beliefs.

Exercise 9-7

1. *The simpler and more conservative theory*: part of the natural cycle of the disease.
3. *The more conservative theory*: a last-minute blitz of TV ads. The theories seem about equal in simplicity.
5. *The more conservative theory*: a big change in the leadership of the government. The theories seem about equal in simplicity.
6. *The more conservative theory*: the result of taking LSD. (Allergy attacks do not normally result in "bizarre and dangerous behavior.") The theories seem about equal in simplicity.
8. *The simpler and more conservative theory*: mandatory immunization.

Exercise 9-8

1. *The most plausible theory:* poison in the drinking water.
2. *The most plausible theory:* rumors of a recession.
4. *The most plausible theory:* the work of clever Egyptian engineers and many slaves.
5. *The most plausible theory:* an increase in the amount of fat consumed by women over age 45.

Exercise 9-9

No answers provided. Requires a unique student response.

Exercise 9-10

No answers provided. Requires a unique student response.

TEST BANK

Multiple Choice
(Correct answers are marked with an asterisk.)

1. A theoretical explanation is a theory, or hypothesis, that tries to explain…
    a. How something is done or how an action is carried out.
    b. The purpose of something, how it functions, or how it fits into a plan.
    c. The meaning of terms or states of affairs.
    * d. Why something is the way it is, why something is the case, or why something happened.

2. Inference to the best explanation is a form of inductive reasoning in which we reason from premises about a state of affairs to…
    a. A deductive conclusion
    * b. An explanation for that state of affairs
    c. An enumerative induction
    d. An analogical induction

3. Before evaluating a theory, we should make sure that it meets the minimum requirement of…
    a. Validity
    b. Cogency
    c. Conservatism
    * d. Consistency

4. A theory that is internally consistent is free of…
    a. Content
    * b. Contradictions
    c. External data
    d. Qualifications

5. The standards used to judge the worth of explanatory theories are known as …
    * a. The criteria of adequacy
    b. The rules of consistency
    c. The criteria of evaluation
    d. The norms of theory

6. If there is some way to determine whether a theory is true or false, it is said to be…
    a. Transparent
    b. Simple
    c. Fruitful
    * d. Testable

7. A theory with scope is one that explains or predicts phenomena....
   a. That it was introduced to explain in the first place
   b. Visible to the naked eye
   * c. Other than that which it was introduced to explain
   d. That are unknown

8. A hypothesis that cannot be verified independently of the phenomenon it's supposed to explain is said to be...
   a. Simple
   * b. *Ad hoc*
   c. Fruitful
   d. Incoherent

9. The second step in the TEST formula is...
   a. Check the premises.
   b. State the theory and check for consistency.
   c. Scrutinize alternative theories.
   * d. Assess the evidence for the theory.

10. A fruitful theory is one that...
   a. Makes the most sense
   b. Makes the fewest assumptions
   c. Makes conservative predictions
   * d. Makes novel predictions

True/False
(Correct answers marked with an asterisk.)

1. The logical pattern for inference to the best explanation is:
   Phenomenon Q.
   E provides the best explanation for Q.
   Therefore, it is probable that E is true.
   * a. True
   b. False

2. A theory that is externally consistent is consistent with the data it's supposed to explain—it fully accounts for the phenomenon to be explained.
   *a. True
   b. False

3. A theory's strangeness is a good reason to discount it.
   a. True
   *b. False

4. A good strategy for evaluating theories is to weigh the evidence for each theory, and the theory with the most evidence wins.
    a. True
    * b. False

5. The criteria of adequacy are used by logicians but not scientists.
    a. True
    * b. False

6. The best theory is the eligible theory that meets the criteria of adequacy better than any of its competitors.
    * a. True
    b. False

7. The moral fault theory of disease is untestable.
    * a. True
    b. False

8. Other things being equal, theories that successfully predict previously unknown phenomena are more credible than those that don't.
    * a. True
    b. False

9. Scientists always reject theories that conflict with their established beliefs.
    a. True
    *b. False

10. There is a strict formula for applying the criteria of adequacy.
    a. True
    *b. False

Short Answer/Short Essay

1. What is the TEST formula? How is it applied to theories?

2. In inference to the best explanation, why should we always consider alternative theories?

3. What is inference to the best explanation and how does it differ from enumerative inductions?

4. What is a theoretical explanation and how does it differ from teleological explanations?

5. Under what circumstances should an inference to the best explanation be considered inductively strong?

6. What is the minimum requirement of consistency? What is the difference between internal and external consistency?

7. What is an untestable theory and why aren't untestable theories useful?

8. Why is the simplest theory less likely to be false?

9. What is an *ad hoc* hypothesis? Why do *ad hoc* hypotheses always make a theory less simple?

10. Why are conservative theories more likely to be true than ones that aren't conservative?

Chapter 10
Judging Scientific Theories

This chapter continues the coverage of inference to the best explanation but shifts the focus to scientific theories and controversial explanations such as those relating to the paranormal. In addition, the basics are here too—discussions of the nature and scope of science, scientific method, the logic of scientific testing, and common errors in research and theory choice.

The first third or so of this chapter can stand alone without help from Chapter 9. Students can jump into this material without getting lost or confused. But students will appreciate the other two-thirds more if they have already worked through Chapter 9.

Like the preceding chapter, this one emphasizes applying the four-step procedure (the TEST formula) to assess competing theories. Four extended examples illustrate how such assessments are done (and have been done in the history of science): (1) geocentric vs. the heliocentric theories of planetary motion, (2) creationism vs. evolution, (3) theories of crop-circle creation, and (4) theories promoted by psychics who claim to communicate with the dead. Again, the natural accompaniment to all this is the writing assignments, essay questions, or class discussions that challenge students to evaluate theories for themselves.

CHAPTER SUMMARY

Science seeks knowledge and understanding of reality, and it does so through the formulation, testing, and evaluation of theories. Science is a way of searching for truth. Technology, though, is the production of products. Science is not a worldview, and we can't identify it with a particular ideology. A particular worldview may predominate in the scientific community, but this doesn't mean that the worldview is what science is all about. Science is not scientism—it is not the only way to acquire knowledge. It is, however, our most reliable way of acquiring knowledge of empirical facts.

The scientific method cannot be identified with any particular set of experimental or observational procedures. But it does involve several general steps: (1) identifying the problem, (2) devising a hypothesis, (3) deriving a test implication, (4) performing the test, and (5) accepting or rejecting the hypothesis.

This kind of theory-testing is part of a broader effort to evaluate a theory against its competitors. This kind of evaluation always involves, implicitly or explicitly, the criteria of adequacy.

Inference to the best explanation can be used to assess weird theories as well as more commonplace explanations in science and everyday life. However, when people try to evaluate extraordinary theories, they often make certain typical mistakes. They may believe that because they can't think of a natural explanation, a paranormal explanation must be correct. They may mistake what seems for what is, forgetting that we shouldn't accept the evidence provided by personal experience if we have good reason to doubt it. And they may not fully understand the concepts of logical and physical possibility. In both science and everyday life, the TEST formula enables us to fairly appraise the worth of all sorts of weird theories, including those about crop circles and communication with the dead, the two cases we examined in this chapter.

EXERCISES NOT ANSWERED IN THE TEXT

Exercise 10-1

1. In general, science is a way of searching for truth; technology is the production of products.

2. The scientific method is a way of systematically assessing the worth of hypotheses. It cannot, however, be identified with any particular set of experimental or observational procedures.

3. No. At any given time, a particular worldview may predominate in the scientific community, but this fact doesn't mean that the worldview is what science is all about.

4. One definition of *scientism* is the view that science is the only reliable way to acquire knowledge.

5. Science embodies to a high degree what is essential to reliable knowing of empirical facts: systematic consideration of alternative solutions or theories, rigorous testing of them, and careful checking and rechecking of the conclusions.

7. No. Induction cannot be the way that most hypotheses are formulated because they often contain concepts that aren't in the data.

8. Deriving a test implication from a hypothesis is a matter of figuring out what a hypothesis implies or predicts. Scientists ask, "If this hypothesis were true, what consequences would follow? What phenomena or events would have to obtain?"

10.
If H, then C.
C.
Therefore, H.

11. No. No hypothesis can ever be conclusively confirmed because it's always possible that we will someday find evidence that undermines or conflicts with the evidence we have now.

13. No. Creationism doesn't fare as well as evolution does when these theories are judged by the criteria of adequacy.

Exercise 10-2

1. *Hypothesis*: Women are more studious than men. *Test implication*: If women are more scientifically literate than men because they are more studious, then a test of scientific literacy that ensures that men and women subjects are equally studious should show men an women performing about the same.

3. *Hypothesis*: Teenage boys have higher rates of automobile crashes because they are inexperienced drivers. *Test implication*: If teenage boys have higher rates of automobile crashes because they are inexperienced drivers, then in a study comparing teen boys with little driving

experience and teen boys with much more driving experience (through drivers training classes, for example), the inexperienced boys should have their usually high rates of crashes while the experienced boys should have lower rates.

4. *Hypothesis*: All the world's terrorists died on September 11, and their ranks have not been replenished. *Test implication*: If all the world's terrorists died on September 11 and their ranks remain unreplenished, then solid intelligence should suggest that there are now no living terrorists anywhere.

5. *Hypothesis*: Some intelligence agents are incompetent. *Test implication*: If intelligence agents who supplied the information are incompetent, then a review of their past and current work should reveal a pattern of incompetent intelligence gathering.

7. *Hypothesis*: B vitamins can lower the incidence of headaches. *Test implication*: If B vitamins really can lower the incidence of headaches, then a double-blind controlled trial (testing B vitamins against placebo in people prone to headaches) should reveal fewer headaches in the experimental group.

8. *Hypothesis*: Diets high in saturated fats are the cause of coronary artery disease. *Test implication*: If diets high in saturated fats are the cause of coronary artery disease, then a double-blind controlled trial comparing the effects of a high-fat diet against a low-fat or normal-fat diet should show a greater incidence of coronary artery disease in the high-fat group.

9. *Hypothesis*: John's home was burglarized. *Test implication*: If John's home was burglarized, then his hidden video cameras positioned inside and outside his house should have captured the burglar on tape breaking the lock and taking the TV.

10. *Hypothesis*: In 2004, rampant unemployment forced many more households into poverty. *Test implication*: If rampant unemployment really has forced many more households into poverty (and has thus widened the gap between the very rich and the very poor), then there should be a strong correlation between unemployment and both reduced unemployed household income and a subsequent rich-poor income gap.

Exercise 10-3

No answers provided. Requires a unique student response.

Exercise 10-4

1. *Test implication*: If Elise has the power to move physical objects with her mind alone, then she should be able to pass a controlled test in which she is supposed to move a small object without using ordinary means (and in which cheating and chance are ruled out). The test would likely disconfirm the theory.

3. *Test implication*: If the Ultra-Sonic 2000 can rid a house of roaches by emitting a particular sound frequency, then the device should pass a series of controlled tests. In each test, two

identical rooms full of roaches could be used, one containing a working Ultra-Sonic 2000, and the other having no anti-roach measures at all. To pass the test, the device would have to consistently rid the room of roaches while the other room remained infested. The tests would likely disconfirm the theory. (In similar tests conducted by the federal government, an anti-bug device failed.)

4. *Test implication*: If the Dodge Intrepid is a more fuel-efficient car than any other on the road, then in a series of fuel mileage tests, the Intrepid should get more miles to the gallon than any other car. The tests would likely disconfirm the theory (because the Intrepid is a bigger car than many others on the road).

5. *Test implication*: If TM practitioners can levitate, they should be able to pass a series of controlled tests in which they are supposed to ascend vertically off the ground without using their muscles or any other ordinary means of propulsion. The tests would likely disconfirm the theory. (TM practitioners have never been able to convincingly demonstrate levitation.)

7. *Test implication*: If lemmings really do often commit mass suicide, then carefully documented observations of lemmings over an extended period should produce good evidence that the creatures do occasionally commit mass suicide. Acceptable evidence must rule out other explanations for the lemmings' seemingly suicidal behavior—for example, that they sometimes die en masse because they attempt to swim across bodies of water but accidentally drown instead. The observations would likely disconfirm the theory.

8. *Test implication*: If it's true that the English sparrow will build nests only in trees, then an extensive survey of sparrow behavior should confirm that sparrow nests are built only in trees. The observations would likely disconfirm the theory (for English sparrows have been known to build nests in places other than trees).

Exercise 10-5

No answers provided. Requires a unique student response.

Exercise 10-6

Hypothesis: Large daily doses of vitamin C can increase the survival times of patients with terminal cancer. *Test implication*: If the hypothesis is true, cancer patients taking vitamin C should show increased survival times compared to cancer patients in a placebo group. *Confirmed or disconfirmed*: Disconfirmed.

Exercise 10-7

1. No
2. 42 percent
3. No
5. Just because something seems real doesn't mean that it is.

7. Something is physically possible is it does not violate a law of science. Something is physically impossible if it does violate a law of science.

8. No

9. No. Some things are logically impossible; anything that is logically impossible cannot exist. Therefore, it is not the case then that anything is possible.

10. The TEST formula is a procedure for evaluating the worth of competing theories:

Step 1. State the theory and check for consistency.

Step 2. Assess the evidence for the theory.

Step 3. Scrutinize alternative theories.

Step 4. Test the theories with the criteria of adequacy.

Exercise 10-8

1. *Theory 1*: A waking dream. *Theory 2*: A daydream *Theory 3*: A real disembodied spirit.

3. *Theory 1*: Coincidence. *Theory 2*: Selective attention. *Theory 3*: "Synchronicity."

4. *Theory 1*: A real, completely normal person who rendered aid then left. *Theory 2*: A real person who rendered aid, gave his name, stayed for awhile—but the person needing help couldn't recall these explanatory details later. *Theory 3*: The stranger was a real guardian angel.

5. *Theory 1*: Some people believe because of stories they've heard. *Theory 2*: Some people believe because they've seen a misleading television program on ghosts. *Theory 3*: Some people have seen real ghosts.

6. *Theory 1*: Coincidence. *Theory 2*: Self-fulfilling prophecy *Theory 3*: Horoscopes accurately predict the future.

8. *Theory 1*: Eleanor has epilepsy. *Theory 2*: Eleanor is mentally ill. *Theory 3*: Eleanor is possessed by demons.

9. *Theory 1*: Pareidolia. *Theory 2*: Expectancy. (Nelly had heard about a famous case it which another woman saw the face of Jesus in a tortilla, so she was on the lookout for a similar miracle in her own tortillas.) *Theory 3*: It's a miracle.

10. *Theory 1*: Intense fear and stress caused by hearing about the spell distracted Ali, causing him to slip on the rocks. *Theory 2*: Coincidence. *Theory 3*: The magical power of the spell caused Ali to break his arm.

Exercise 10-9

No answers provided. Requires a unique student response.

Exercise 10-10

No answers provided. Requires a unique student response.

TEST BANK

Multiple Choice
(Correct answers are marked with an asterisk.)

1. The first step in the scientific method is...
   a. Observe.
   b. Derive a test implication or prediction.
   * c. Identify the problem or pose a question.
   d. Perform a test.

2. When scientists ask, "If this hypothesis were true, what consequences would follow?" they are trying to identify a...
   a. Theory
   * b. Test implication
   c. Hypothesis
   d. Rationale

3. The conditional argument that expresses the logical pattern of disconfirming a hypothesis is called...
   a. *Modus ponens*
   b. Denying the antecedent
   c. Affirming the consequent
   * d. *Modus tollens*

4. Neither the subjects nor the experimenters know who receives the real treatment in this kind of study...
   * a. Double-blind
   b. Single-blind
   c. Replicated
   d. Confirmed

5. The standards used to judge the worth of scientific theories are known as ...
   a. The rules of consistency
   b. The criteria of evaluation
   * a. The criteria of adequacy
   d. The scientific method

6. Compared to Ptolemy's geocentric theory, Copernicus's heliocentric theory was...
   a. More conservative
   b. Superior in scope
   c. More complicated
   * d. Simpler

118

7. Both creationism and evolution are....
    a. Conservative
    * b. Testable
    c. Untestable
    d. Fruitful

8. The fallacious leap to a non-natural explanation for a phenomena is an example of the fallacy of ...
    * a. Appeal to ignorance
    b. Begging the question
    c. Straw man
    d. Division

9. ESP, UFOs, and dowsing are...
    a. Logically impossible
    * b. Logically possible
    c. Logically invalid
    d. Logically strong

10. The theory that crop circles are made by space aliens is ...
    a. Has scope
    b. Fruitful
    c. Conservative
    * d. Not simple

True/False
(Correct answers marked with an asterisk.)

1. Regardless of their authenticity, the performances of psychics who claim to communicate with the dead seem to be indistinguishable from those based on cold reading.
    * a. True
    b. False

2. Science is our only reliable way to acquire knowledge..
    a. True
    *b. False

3. The last step in the scientific method is to accept or reject the hypothesis.
    *a. True
    b. False

4. Scientific hypotheses are derived inductively.
    a. True
    * b. False

5. Hypotheses can be conclusively confirmed.
    a. True
    * b. False

6. If the results of a scientific study are questionable, then replication is not necessary.
    a. True
    *b. False

7. Ultimately, scientists accepted the Copernican model over Ptolemy's because of its endorsement by the Vatican.
    a. True
    *b. False

8. Evolution has yielded some novel predictions.
    * a. True
    b. False

9. According to the text, no one has ever seen evolution.
    a. True
    *b. False

10. Scientists do not test weird theories.
    a. True
    *b. False

Short Answer/Short Essay

1. Is science ideology? Why or why not?

2. Why is science such a reliable way to acquire knowledge?

3. What are the five steps in the scientific method?

4. Can the scientific method be identified with any particular set of experimental or observational procedures? Why or why not?

5. Why do scientists derive a test implications from hypotheses?

6. What conditional arguments are used in the testing of hypotheses?

7. Why can't hypotheses be conclusively confuted?

8. What might be the basic elements of a scientific study to test the efficacy of a new migraine medication?

9. According to the text, why should anyone bother to evaluate weird claims?

10. According to the text, what is probably the most common error in assessing paranormal claims?

Chapter 11
Judging Moral Arguments and Theories

This chapter covers three major topics: moral arguments, moral theories, and worldviews—all of which are conceptually linked by earlier chapters. For the most part, the sections on these topics are modular so that students can profitably work through any one of them and disregard the other two. On the other hand, if students are to delve into all three, the present order of the topics will probably make good sense to them, unfolding mostly in a progressive way.

The material on theories and worldviews will probably come much easier to students if they have already absorbed at least one of the other two inference-to-the-best-explanation chapters (Chapters 9 and 10). And the section on moral reasoning will seem straightforward to students if they have already worked through one of the earlier chapters on arguments.

CHAPTER SUMMARY

A moral argument is an argument in which the conclusion is a moral statement. A moral statement is a statement asserting that an action is right or wrong (moral or immoral) or that a person or motive is good or bad. In a moral argument, we cannot establish the conclusion without a moral premise. A standard moral argument has at least one premise that asserts a general moral principle, at least one premise that is a nonmoral claim, and a conclusion that is a moral statement. Often a moral premise in a moral argument is implicit. In evaluating any moral argument, it's best to specify any implicit premises. The best approach to identifying the implicit premises is to treat moral arguments as deductive. Your job then is to supply plausible premises that will make the argument valid. You can test a premise that is a general moral principle by trying to think of counterexamples to it.

Theories of morality are attempts to explain what makes an action right or what makes a person good. We test moral theories the same way we test any other theory—by applying criteria of adequacy to a theory and its competitors. The criteria of adequacy for moral theories are (1) consistency with considered moral judgments, (2) consistency with our experience of the moral life, and (3) workability in real-life situations.

Making a coherent worldview is the work of a lifetime. Worldviews are composites of theories, including theories of morality. A good worldview must consist of good theories. But it also must be have internal consistency—the theories composing our worldview must not conflict.

EXERCISES NOT ANSWERED IN THE TEXT

Exercise 11-1

1. A moral theory is an explanation of what makes an action right or what makes a person good. It tries to specify what all right actions and all good things have in common.

2. A worldview is a philosophy of life, a set of beliefs and theories that help us make sense of a wide range of issues in life.

3. A moral statement is a statement asserting that an action is right or wrong (moral or immoral) or that something (such as a person or motive) is good or bad.

4. In a moral argument, at least one premise is a moral statement that asserts a general moral principle or moral standard. At least one premise makes a nonmoral claim. And the conclusion is a moral statement, or judgment, about a particular case (usually a particular kind of action).

6. Implicit moral premises are often dubious and need to be studied closely. General moral principles that are taken for granted may turn out to be unfounded or incomplete.

7. We often can assess a general moral principle by trying to think of counterexamples to it.

8. Moral judgments are decisions about the morality of specific classes of actions or of the goodness of people and their motives.

10. (1) consistency with considered moral judgments, (2) consistency with our experience of the moral life, and (3) workability in real-life situations.

11. Like scientific theories, moral theories must be consistent with all relevant data, consistent with background information, and helpful in solving problems.

12. Jeremy Bentham

Exercise 11-2

2. Nonmoral
3. Moral
4. Nonmoral
5. Moral
7. Moral
8. Nonmoral
10. Moral

Exercise 11-3

1. People should keep their promises; Noah promised to drive Thelma to Los Angeles; so he should stop bellyaching and do it.

2. The authorities have a moral obligation to intervene when refugees are being shot at and lied to. The refugees were shot at and lied to, and the authorities did nothing to stop any of this. The authorities should have intervened.

3. The United States is justified in invading another country only when that country poses and imminent threat. There was never any imminent threat from the Iraqi government, so the United States should not have invaded Iraq.

5. Anyone who uses a gun in the commission of a crime deserves to receive a long prison sentence. Burton used a gun in the commission of a crime; therefore he should get a long prison term.

6. Anyone who knows that murder is going to take place has a moral obligation to try to stop it. Ellen knew that a murder was going to take place. It was her duty to try to stop it. (Often people who would put forth an argument like this would also assume that a person is obligated to intervene only if it's physically *possible* for him or her to intervene.)

7. Any procedure that is unnatural should not be permitted to be used on people. In vitro fertilization is unnatural. Ahmed should never have allowed his daughter to receive in vitro fertilization.

8. Doctors should never experiment on people without their consent. The doctors performed the experiment on twenty patients without their consent. Obviously, that was wrong.

10. If someone does another person a favor (performs a service for no pay), that other person is obligated to return the favor by doing a minimum service ("the least you can do"). Ling spent all day weeding Mrs. Black's garden for no pay. The least Mrs. Black should do is let Ling borrow some gardening tools.

Exercise 11-4

1. *Counterexample*: Taking an aspirin is unnatural. Is taking an aspirin therefore immoral?

2. *Counterexample*: What if by telling a little lie you could save the lives of a million people? Would telling that lie be wrong?

4. *Counterexample*: What if your mother and several complete strangers are trapped inside a burning building and are about to die, and you can rescue only one of them? Would it be wrong for you to value your mother's life over all the others and rescue her?

5. *Counterexample*: Suppose a serial killer decides to do something in his own best interests—kill three police officers who are pursuing him. Is he therefore justified in doing such a thing?

6. *Counterexample*: Suppose your society approves of enslaving a million of your fellow citizens, as some societies have actually done. Is this mass slavery therefore moral?

8. *Counterexample*: Hitler approved of the murder of millions of Jews. Was such mass murder therefore morally right?

9. *Counterexample*: Suppose you promise a friend that you will meet her for lunch, but on the way to lunch you witness a terrible automobile accident and are in a position to save the lives of ten people (and there's no one else around to help). If you help the accident victims you will break your promise to your friend. Are you really morally obligated to keep your promise?

10. *Counterexample*: Let's say that for religious reasons you decide to blow up a public building. Is such an act then morally acceptable?

Exercise 11-5

1.
It is immoral to do harm to others.
The movie *Lorenzo's Oil* does harm to others by giving people false hope about a deadly disease and by misleading people about the medical facts.
The movie is therefore immoral (or, those who produced and promoted the movie have acted immorally).

2.
Regardless of whether the victims are Muslim or not, the vicious murder of innocent human beings is reprehensible and repugnant, an affront to everything Islam stands for.
Al Qaeda has viciously murdered innocent human beings—both Muslim and non-Muslim.
Therefore, these acts committed by Al Qaeda are reprehensible and repugnant.
No one should have any sympathy for an organization that murders innocent human beings.
Therefore, the Saudis should have had no sympathy for Al Qaeda after the May bombings.

3.
Above all other concerns, parents have a duty to ensure the health and safety of their children and to use whatever means are most likely to secure those benefits.
The Joneses ignored this basic moral principle (failed to ensure the health and safety of their child and to use whatever means are most likely to secure those benefits).
Therefore, the Joneses acted immorally (and deserve whatever punishment the state deems appropriate).

Exercise 11-6

1. The theory seems consistent with a great many of our considered moral judgments. It is not clear whether the theory is consistent with our judgments regarding the punishment of criminals or acts of war. Because of the stipulation "everyone considered," the theory appears to be inconsistent with the notion of having stronger obligations to one's family than to "all persons equally." This theory seems to imply, for example, that we should give equal love and consideration to everyone in a burning building when we are trying to decide who to rescue— even though one of them is our mother and the rest are strangers.

2. The theory seems consistent with our experience of the moral life. It implies that moral judgments are possible, that we can have moral disagreements, and that we can sometimes act immorally.

3. The theory does not seem to be workable. It offers us no help in resolving the moral dilemmas listed:

(1) Your beloved mother has a terminal illness which causes her unimaginable pain, and she begs you to kill her.

(2) You promise to buy your beloved spouse a car, but a half dozen homeless people beg you to give them the money that you had set aside for the car.

(3) You are a doctor who must decide which of one hundred patients should receive a life-saving organ transplant. You can choose only one, though you love all of them. Some are elderly; some, in great pain; some, very young; and some, Nobel laureates.

4. This theory is consistent with many of our considered moral judgments. Unlike act-utilitarianism, it does not seem to sanction obviously immoral acts. But that may be because the theory has nothing to say about countless situations that call for a moral decision. That's the main problem: The theory, as described in the exercise, is unworkable. Many (most?) moral dilemmas simply cannot be resolved by a general appeal to love. This extreme unworkability makes it difficult to call the theory "good." Perhaps the kindest description is that it is incomplete.

TEST BANK

Multiple Choice
(Correct answers are marked with an asterisk.)

1. A set of beliefs and theories that help us make sense of a wide range of issues in life is known as a...
      a. Theory
      * b. Worldview
      c. Premise
      d. Morality

2. The view that moral statements are not statements at all is called...
      a. Relativism
      b. Ethical egoism
      c. Absolutism
      * d. Emotivism

3. A statement asserting that an action is right or wrong (moral or immoral) or that something (such as a person or motive) is good or bad is a...
      *a. Moral statement
      b. Amoral statement
      c. Nonmoral statement
      d. Motivating statement

4. In a standard moral argument, it is not possible to establish the conclusion (a moral statement) without a moral…
    a. Theory
    b. Worldview
    * c. Premise
    d. Deduction

5. The best approach to identifying implicit premises in a moral argument is to treat the arguments as …
    a. Inductive
    b. Invalid
    c. Cogent
    * d. Deductive

6. One way to evaluate a moral premise is to try to …
    * a. Think of counterexamples to it.
    b. Think of an alternative premise.
    c. Rephrase the premise.
    d. Ignore counterexamples to it.

7. Moral judgments are usually justified by appeals to…
    a. Nonmoral statements
    b. General emotive states
    * c. General moral principles
    d. Considered desires

8. Cultural relativism is the view that what makes an action right is that it is…
    a. Approved by oneself
    * b. Approved by one's culture
    c. Conforms to universal moral standards
    d. In one's best interests

9. According to the text, to identify the best moral theory, we must compare competing theories and evaluate them using the…
    a. Accepted moral norms
    * b. Moral criteria of adequacy
    c. Scientific criteria of adequacy
    d. Next best theory

10. One of three criteria for judging the worth of moral theories is consistency with …
    a. Social norms
    b. all moral theories
    c. Considered nonmoral judgments
    * d. Considered moral judgments

True/False
(Correct answers marked with an asterisk.)

1. According to the text, moral agents should strive to achieve a "reflective equilibrium" between facts and theory.
	* a. True
	b. False

2. Our moral experience may involve making moral judgments, but it does not include having moral disagreements.
	a. True
	*b. False

3. What matters most in act-utilitarianism is whether a moral law is broken.
	a. True
	* b. False

4. A crucial criterion for judging a worldview is internal consistency.
	* a. True
	b. False

5. Nonmoral statements assert that something is right or wrong, good or bad.
	a. True
	* b. False

6. In a moral argument, we cannot infer what *should be* or *ought to be* (in the conclusion) from statements about *what is*.
	* a. True
	b. False

7. Both plausible scientific theories and plausible moral theories must be conservative.
	* a. True
	b. False

8. According to act-utilitarianism, if two actions produce exactly the same amount of overall happiness, one of the actions must be wrong.
	a. True
	*b. False

9. According to the text, if the theories that make up our worldview are inconsistent with one another, there is something wrong with our worldview.
	* a. True
	b. False

10. A moral argument can be devised without including any moral premises.
    a. True
    *b. False

Short Answer/Short Essay

1. What is the basic structure of a moral argument?

2. What is the difference between a moral and a nonmoral premise?

3. How does one go about identifying an implicit premise in a moral argument?

4. Why is it important to identify implicit premises?

5. According to the text, what are some problematic implications of subjective relativism?

6. According to the text, what are some problematic implications of cultural relativism?

7. What are the moral criteria of adequacy?

8. What does it mean for a moral theory to be consistent with our experience of the moral life?

9. According to the text, how is act-utilitarianism inconsistent with our considered moral judgments?

10. According to the text, what is one way to determine whether a general moral principle is true?

Outline of PowerPoint Slides
(slides available at www.oup.com/us/criticalthinking)

Chapter 1

[Slide 1]

Critical thinking:

The systematic evaluation or formulation of beliefs, or statements, by rational standards.

- *systematic*—because it involves distinct procedures and methods.
- *evaluation* and *formulation*—used to assess existing beliefs and devise new ones.
- *rational standards*—beliefs are judged by how well they are supported by reasons.

[Slide 2]

To critically examine your beliefs is to critically examine your life, for your beliefs in large measure define your life.

Socrates: "The unexamined life is not worth living."

[Slide 3]

Statement (claim): An assertion that something is or is not the case.

Premise: A statement given in support of another statement.

Conclusion: A statement that premises are used to support.

Argument: A group of statements in which some of them (the premises) are intended to support another of them (the conclusion).

[Slide 4]

Some premise indicator words: because, since, in view of the fact, given that, for the reason that, due to the fact that.

Some conclusion indicator words: therefore, thus, so, consequently, it follows that, we can conclude that, ergo, hence.

Chapter 2

[Slide 5]

Common impediments to critical thinking:

Category 1—hindrances that arise because of *how* we think.

Category 2—hindrances that occur because of *what* we think.

[Slide 6]

Self-interested thinking—accepting a claim solely on the grounds that it advances, or coincides with, our interests.

Overcoming self-interested thinking:

- Watch out when things get very personal.

- Beware of the urge to distort your thinking to save face.

- Be alert to ways that critical thinking can be undermined.

- Ensure that nothing has been left out.

- Avoid selective attention.

- Look for opposing evidence.

[Slide 7]

Group Thinking:

- *peer pressure*—appeal to the masses (appeal to popularity), appeal to common practice, prejudice, bias, racism.

- *stereotyping*—drawing conclusions about people without sufficient reasons.

[Slide 8]

Subjective relativism—The view that truth depends solely on what someone believes; truth is relative to persons.

Social relativism—The view that truth is relative to societies.

Problems with these views--

- They imply that persons and societies are infallible.
- They are self-defeating.

[Slide 9]

Philosophical skepticism—The view that we know much less than we think we know or nothing at all.

1. One form of this view says that knowledge requires certainty.

2. If knowledge requires certainty, we know very little.

3. But we sometimes do seem to have knowledge—even though we do not have absolutely conclusive reasons.

Chapter 3

[Slide 10]

Deductive Arguments

- A deductive argument is intended to provide <u>conclusive support</u> for its conclusion.

- A deductive argument that succeeds in providing conclusive support for its premise is said to be <u>valid</u>. A valid argument is such that if its premises are true, its conclusion <u>must be true</u>.

- A deductively valid argument with true premises is said to be <u>sound</u>.

[Slide 11]

Inductive Arguments

- An inductive argument is intended to provide <u>probable support</u> for its conclusion.

- An inductive argument that succeeds in providing probable support for its conclusion is said to be <u>strong</u>. A strong argument is such that if its premises are true, its conclusion is <u>probably true</u>.

- An inductively strong argument with true premises is said to be <u>cogent</u>.

[Slide 12]

Judging Arguments—telling (1) whether an argument is deductive or inductive and (2) whether it gives good reasons for accepting the conclusion)

Step 1. Find the argument's conclusion and then its premises.

Step 2. Ask: Is it the case that if the premises are true the conclusion *must* be true?

Step 3. Ask: Is it the case that if the premises are true, its conclusion is *probably* true?

Step 4. Ask: Is the argument intended to offer conclusive or probable support for its conclusion but *fails* to do so?

[Slide 13]

Finding implicit premises:

Step 1. Search for a credible premise that would make the argument *valid*. Choose the supplied premise that **(a) is most plausible** and **(b) fits best with the author's intent.**

Step 2. Search for a credible premise that would make the argument as *strong* as possible. Choose the supplied premise that fulfills stipulations a. and b. above.

Step 3. Evaluate the reconstituted argument.

[Slide 14]

Valid Conditional Argument Forms

Affirming the Antecedent (**Modus Ponens***)*	*Denying the Consequent (***Modus Tollens***)*
If p, *then* q. p. *Therefore,* q.	*If* p, *then* q. *Not* q. *Therefore, not* p.
Example:	*Example:*
If Spot barks, a burglar is in the house. Spot is barking. Therefore, a burglar is in the house.	If Spot barks, a burglar is in the house. A burglar is not in the house. Therefore, Spot is not barking.

[Slide 15]

Valid Conditional Argument Form

Hypothetical Syllogism

If p, *then* q.
If q, *then* r.
Therefore, if p, *then* r.

Example:

If Ajax steals the money, he will go to jail.
If Ajax goes to jail, his family will suffer.
Therefore, if Ajax steals the money, his family will suffer.

[Slide 16]

Diagramming Arguments: Step by Step

1. Underline all premise or conclusion indicator words such as "since," "therefore," and "because." Then number the statements.

2. Find the conclusion and draw a wavy line under it.

3. Locate the premises and underline them.

4. Cross out all extraneous material—redundancies, irrelevant sentences, questions, exclamations.

5. Draw the diagram, connecting premises and conclusions with arrows showing logical connections. Include both dependent and independent premises.

Chapter 4

[Slide 17]

When Claims Conflict…

- *If a claim conflicts with other claims we have good reason to accept, we have good grounds for doubting it.*

- *If a claim conflicts with our background information, we have good reason to doubt it.*

[Slide 18]

Belief and Evidence

- *We should proportion our belief to the evidence.*

- *It's not reasonable to believe a claim when there is no good reason for doing so.*

Experts and Evidence

- *If a claim conflicts with expert opinion, we have good reason to doubt it.*

- *When the experts disagree about a claim, we have good reason to doubt it.*

[Slide 20]

Personal Experience

- *It's reasonable to accept the evidence provided by personal experience only if there's no good reason to doubt it.*

Factors that can give us good reason to doubt the reliability of personal experience:

- Impairment
- Expectation
- Innumeracy

[Slide 21]

How we fool ourselves:

- Resisting contrary evidence
- Looking for confirming evidence
- Preferring available evidence

[Slide 22]

How to evaluate the reliability of the news::

- **Consider whether the report conflicts with what you have good reason to believe.**
- **Look for reporter slanting.**
- **Consider the source.**
- **Check for missing information.**
- **Look for false emphasis.**
- **Check alternative news sources.**

Chapter 5

[Slide 23]

Two categories of fallacies:

Category 1—Fallacies that have *irrelevant* premises.

Category 2—Fallacies that have *unacceptable* premises.

[Slide 24]

genetic fallacy—arguing that a claim is true or false solely because of its origin.

Example: We should reject that proposal for solving the current welfare mess. It comes straight from the Democratic Party.

composition—arguing that what is true of the parts must be true of the whole.

Example: The atoms that make up the human body are invisible. Therefore, the human body is invisible.

division—arguing that what is true of the whole must be true of the parts.

Example: This machine is heavy. Therefore, all the parts of this machine are heavy.

[Slide 25]

appeal to the person (or *ad hominem*, meaning "to the man")—rejecting a claim by criticizing the person who makes it rather than the claim itself.

Example: We should reject Chen's argument for life on other planets. He dabbles in the paranormal.

Types:

- Personal attack
- Accusation of inconsistency
- *Tu quoque*
- Circumstances
- Poisoning the well

[Slide 26]

equivocation—the use of a word in two different senses in an argument.

Example: Only man is rational. No woman is a man. Therefore, no woman is rational.

appeal to the masses—arguing that a claim must be true merely because a substantial number of people believe it.

Example: Of course the war is justified. Everyone believes that it's justified.

appeal to tradition—arguing that a claim must be true just because it's part of a tradition.

Example: Acupuncture has been used for a thousand years in China. It must work.

[Slide 27]

appeal to ignorance—arguing that a lack of evidence proves something. *Examples*:

- No one has shown that ghosts aren't real, so they must be real.

- No one has shown that ghosts are real, so they must not exist.

[Slide 28]

appeal to emotion—the use of emotions as premises in an argument.

Example: You should hire me for this network analyst position. I'm the best person for the job. If I don't get a job soon my wife will leave me, and I won't have enough money to pay for my mother's heart operation. Come on, give me a break

red herring—the deliberate raising of an irrelevant issue during an argument.

Example: Every woman should have the right to an abortion on demand. There's no question about it. These anti-abortion activists block the entrances to abortion clinics, threaten abortion doctors, and intimidate anyone who wants to terminate a pregnancy.

[Slide 29]

straw man—the distorting, weakening, or oversimplifying of someone's position so it can be more easily attacked or refuted.

Example: Senator Kennedy is opposed to the military spending bill, saying that it's too costly. Why does he always want to slash everything to the bone? He wants a pint-sized military that couldn't fight off a crazed band of terrorists, let alone a rogue nation.

[Slide 30]

begging the question (or arguing in a circle)—the attempt to establish the conclusion of an argument by using that conclusion as a premise.

Example: God exists. We know that God exists because the Bible says so, and we should believe what the Bible says because God wrote it.

false dilemma—asserting that there are only two alternatives to consider when there are actually more than two.

Example: Look, either you support the war or you are a traitor to your country. You don't support the war. So you're a traitor.

slippery slope—arguing, without good reasons, that taking a particular step will inevitably lead to a further, undesirable step (or steps).

Example: We absolutely must not lose the war in Vietnam. If South Vietnam falls to the communists, then Thailand will fall to them. If Thailand falls to them, then South Korea will fall to them. And before you know it, all of Southeast Asia will be under communist control.

[Slide 32]

hasty generalization—drawing a conclusion about a whole group based on an inadequate sample of the group.

Example: The only male professor I've had this year was a chauvinist pig. All the male professors at this school must be chauvinist pigs.

faulty analogy—an argument in which the things being compared are not sufficiently similar in relevant ways.

Example: Dogs are warm-blooded, nurse their young, and give birth to puppies. Humans are warm-blooded and nurse their young. Therefore, humans give birth to puppies too.

Chapter 6

[Slide 33]

4 Logical Connectives:

& Conjunction (and)—as in *p & q* (Alice rode her bike, and John walked.)

v Disjunction (or)—as in *p v q* (Either Alice rode her bike, or John walked.)

~ Negation (not)—as in *~p* (Alice did not ride her bike. Or: It is not the case that Alice rode her bike.)

☐ Conditional (if-then)—as in *p ☐ q* (If Alice rode her bike, then John walked.)

[Slide 34]

Truth table for a conjunction:

p	q	p & q
T	T	T
T	F	F
F	T	F
F	F	F

[Slide 35]

Truth table for a disjunction:

p	q	p v q
T	T	T
T	F	T
F	T	T
F	F	F

[Slide 36]

Truth table for a negation:

p	~ p
T	F
F	T

[Slide 37]

Truth table for a conditional:

p	q	p □ q
T	T	T
T	F	F
F	T	T
F	F	T

Chapter 7

[Slide 38]

4 Standard Categorical Statements:

1. *All S are P.* *(All cats are carnivores.)*

2. *No S are P.* *(No cats are carnivores.)*
3. *Some S are P.* *(Some cats are carnivores.)*
4. *Some S are not P.* *(Some cats are not carnivores.)*

[Slide 39]

Quality and *Quantity* *of the 4 Standard Categorical Statements*:

A   *All S are P* (universal affirmative)
E   *No S are P* (universal negative)
I   *Some S are P* (particular affirmative)
O   *Some S are not P* (particular negative)

[Slide 40]

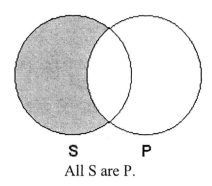

S   P
All S are P.

[Slide 41]

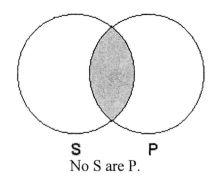

S   P
No S are P.

140

[Slide 42]

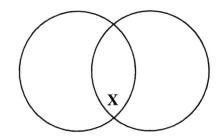

S   **P**
Some S are P.

[Slide 43]

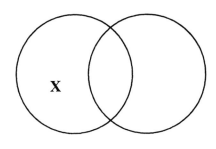

S   **P**
Some S are not P.

[Slide 44]

Categorical Syllogism

Major Premise   1. *[middle term] [major term].*
Minor Premise   2. *[minor term] [middle term].*
Conclusion   3. *Therefore, [minor term] [major term].*

1. *All egomaniacs are warmongers.*
2. *All dictators are egomaniacs.*
3. *Therefore, all dictators are warmongers.*

1. *All M are P.*
2. *All S are M*
3. *Therefore, all S are P.*

Chapter 8

[Slide 45]

Enumerative Induction: An inductive argument pattern in which we reason from premises about individual members of a group to conclusions about the group as a whole.

X percent of the observed members of group A have property P.
Therefore, X percent of all members of group A probably have property P.

[Slide 46]

target group (or target population) In enumerative induction, the whole collection of individuals under study.

sample (or sample member) In enumerative induction, the observed members of the target group.

relevant property (or property in question) In enumerative induction, a property, or characteristic, that is of interest in the target group.

[Slide 47]

hasty generalization The fallacy of drawing a conclusion about a target group based on an inadequate sample size.

biased sample A sample that does not properly represent the target group.

representative sample In enumerative induction, a sample that resembles the target group in all relevant ways.

[Slide 48]

random sample A sample that is selected randomly from a target group in such a way as to ensure that the sample is representative. In a simple random selection, every member of the target group has an equal chance of being selected for the sample.

confidence level In statistical theory, the probability that the sample will accurately represent the target group within the margin of error.

margin of error The variation between the values derived from a sample and the true values of the whole target group.

[Slide 49]

argument by analogy (also, analogical induction) An argument making use of analogy, reasoning that because two or more things are similar in several respects, they must be similar in some further respect.

Thing A has properties P_1, P_2, P_3 plus the property P_4.
Thing B has properties P_1, P_2, and P_3.
Therefore, thing B probably has property P_4.

[Slide 50]

Criteria for judging arguments by analogy:

1. The number of relevant similarities.

2. The number of relevant dissimilarities.

3. The number of instances compared.

4. The diversity among cases.

[Slide 51]

Causal Confusions

Misidentifying relevant factors.

Overlooking relevant factors.

Confusing coincidence with cause.

Confusing cause with temporal order (post hoc fallacy).

Confusing cause and effect.

[Slide 52]

Necessary and Sufficient Conditions

A **necessary condition** for the occurrence of an event is one without which the event cannot occur.

A **sufficient condition** for the occurrence of an event is one that guarantees that the event occurs.

Chapter 9

[Slide 53]

inference to the best explanation A form of inductive reasoning in which we reason from premises about a state of affairs to an explanation for that state of affairs:

> Phenomenon Q.
> E provides the best explanation for Q.
> Therefore, it is probable that E is true.

[Slide 54]

Minimum Requirement: Consistency

Internal consistency—A theory that is internally consistent is free of contradictions.

External consistency—A theory that is externally consistent is consistent with the data it's supposed to explain.

[Slide 55]

Criteria of Adequacy

Testability Whether there is some way to determine if a theory is true.

Fruitfulness The number of novel predictions made.

Scope The amount of diverse phenomena explained.

Simplicity The number of assumptions made.

Conservatism How well a theory fits with existing knowledge.

[Slide 56]

The **TEST formula**:

*Step 1. State the **T**heory and check for consistency.*

*Step 2. Assess the **E**vidence for the theory.*

*Step 3. **S**crutinize alternative theories.*

*Step 4. **T**est the theories with the criteria of adequacy.*

Chapter 10

[Slide 57]

The Scientific Method:

1. Identify the problem or pose a question.

2. Devise a hypothesis to explain the event or phenomenon.

3. Derive a test implication or prediction.

4. Perform the test.

5. Accept or reject the hypothesis.

[Slide 58]

The Logic of Hypothesis Testing:

The hypothesis disconfirmed—

If H, then C.
not-C.
Therefore, not-H.

The hypothesis confirmed—

If H, then C.
C.
Therefore, H.

[Slide 59]

Common Mistakes in Assessing 'Weird' Theories:

1. Believing that just because you can't think of a natural explanation, a phenomenon must be paranormal.

2. Thinking that just because something *seems* real, it *is* real. (A better principle: It's reasonable to accept the evidence provided by personal experience only if there's no good reason to doubt it.)

3. Misunderstanding logical possibility and physical possibility. Also, believing that if something is logically possible, it must be actual.

Chapter 11

[Slide 60]

moral statement: A statement asserting that an action is right or wrong (moral or immoral) or that something (such as a person or motive) is good or bad.

moral statements—

Serena should keep her promise to you.

It is wrong to treat James so harshly.

Abortion is immoral.

[Slide 61]

nonmoral statement: A statement that does not assert that an action is right or wrong (moral or immoral) or that something (such as a person or motive) is good or bad. Nonmoral statements describe states of affairs.

nonmoral statements—

Serena did not keep her promise to you.

James was treated harshly.

Some people think abortion is immoral.

[Slide 62]

Judging Moral Theories

Moral Criteria of Adequacy:

1. Consistency with our considered moral judgments.

2. Consistency with our experience of the moral life.

3. Workability in real-life situations.